From **Primrose Hill** to **Euston Road**

ISBN 0-904491-30-7

From Primrose Hill to Euston Road

a survey of Streets, Buildings and Former Residents in a part of Camden

a revised version of *Primrose Hill to Euston Road* (1988)

Compiled by Camden History Society's Street History Group

Edited by Peter Woodford

Designed by Ivor Kamlish

Contents

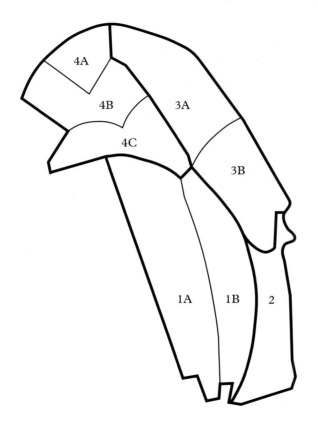

TO USE THIS BOOK you do not need to climb Primrose Hill: it is, like other books in the 'Streets of' series of the Camden History Society, a street survey. Our area extends from the foot of Primrose Hill north-eastwards to Chalk Farm station, then on a broad front roughly southwards to Euston Road. It is, however, very pleasant to walk up the Hill to its lookout point and note some features of the area we survey: glimpses through the trees of the great Nash terraces lining the eastern side of Regent's Park (the Zoological Gardens and the western side being in Westminster), the Regent's Canal at your feet, a Birmingham train heard or sensed behind you as it burrows beneath the Hill, the tall office buildings on the Euston Road; and throughout, the usual London mixture of trees, green spaces, trim residences and hectic commercial activity, the latter exemplified by the 33-storey Euston Tower and its 20-storey neighbour, towering over the few neighbouring Victorian 3-storey houses, likewise dwarfed by the post-war high-rise flats.

We describe the streets - and what we can deduce of their history from directories, insurance maps, poverty maps, picture postcards and other documentary sources – in eight itineraries, each of which starts at or near a Tube station or bus stop. We attempt to point out anything interesting that was visible to the naked eye in 1994, adding where we can what preceded the building or feature you are looking at. Sometimes a piece of history can be gleaned, or at least suspected, just by looking at the building itself, and we have hinted at this kind of information in the text.

With book in hand you may well develop sharper eyes than ours; if you do see anything worthy of note that we have not pointed out please write to the Camden History Society – or, better still, pen a note for its Newsletter. Good hunting!

The 'Primrose Hill Group'
Roger Cline
David and Ruth Hayes
Barbara Scott
Stella Smethurst
Esther Whant
Peter Woodford
Robin and Sonia Woolven

August 1994

Illustrations

The Society thanks Malcolm Holmes
for his ever-helpful assistance and the Camden Local
Studies Library for permission to reproduce items on
pp 10,14,18,20,22,28,34,44,48,54,58,62,66 and 70;
the Camden Bus Estate Agents for the item on p 55;
Roger Cline for the loan of the original Morris panorama
for the cover; Stephen Kamlish for the new maps;
and Ivor Kamlish for the sketches
and the re-design of the whole book.

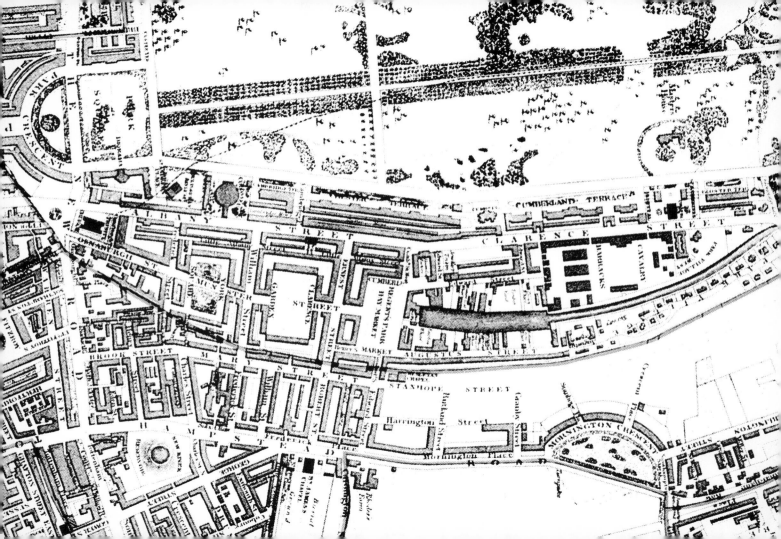

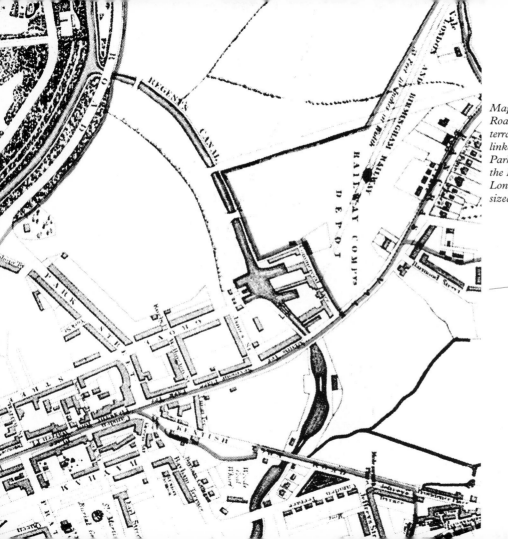

Map of the area as it was in 1834. Euston Road is still 'The New Road'. The Nash terraces in Regent's Park are in place, and are linked to Camden Town by Park Street (now Parkway), but this lay across fields bisected by the Regent's Canal and through which the London-Birmingham railway was to cut a sizeable swathe.

→ N

9

10   *One of the vanished glories of the area: the Colosseum, depicted about 1835 (demolished 1875)*

Historical background

THE AREA COVERED by this book runs from Chalk Farm Underground station in the north, the foot of Primrose Hill and the Broad Walk in Regent's Park on the west, to Euston Road in the south. The eastern boundary is the medieval road which runs northwards from the corner of Euston and Tottenham Court Roads towards Hampstead, now known as Hampstead Road, Camden High Street, and Chalk Farm Road. The northern part of the area lay in the ancient manor of Rugmere, whose manor house was possibly on the site of the Chalk Farm Tavern (in the residential area now known as Primrose Hill), the remainder in Tottenhall Manor, whose manor house acquired the name of Tottenham Court.

In 1668, Charles II granted the lease of Tottenhall Manor to his favourite, Henry Benet, Earl of **Arlington**, whose daughter Isabella married Henry **Fitzroy**, son of Charles II and Barbara Villiers. Henry Fitzroy became first Duke of **Grafton** and Isabella brought the Tottenhall lease with her, and so it came into the possession of the Fitzroy family. (The names that will recur in this book, some of them many times, are shown in boldface.)

In Charles II's time the whole area consisted of farmland, pasture and some woodland, with no habitation at the northern end other than Lower **Chalcot** (see *The Streets of Belsize* for Upper Chalcot). This lay east of Primrose Hill and was joined by a lane to the main Hampstead road. The name Chalcot is synonymous with Chaldecote or Caldecote and in Old English means a cold hut, probably in this instance a shelter for travellers. Lower Chalcot first comes into the record in 1678 as a modest inn attached to a farm. By the mid-18th century, Chalcot's Farm had become Chalk House Farm and so arises the name Chalk Farm – not, as many suppose, because of chalk in the subsoil: it is all heavy clay.

Primrose Hill to the west lay mostly in the Eton Estate, given to Eton College by Henry VI in 1449. To the south a park called, with many variations of spelling, Marybone Park was formed, of which the eastern part lay in St Pancras (now Camden). This is now Regent's Park (section 1A below).

The lease of Tottenhall Manor had by the mid-18th century descended to Charles Fitzroy, great-grandson of Henry and Isabella. In 1768 his elder brother, the third Duke of Grafton, who fortunately happened to be Prime Minister at the time, arranged an Act of Parliament enabling Charles Fitzroy to buy the freehold of the manor from St Paul's. The deal proved a singularly good bargain for the Fitzroys. Charles was created Baron of **Southampton** in 1780 and, in 1786, he rounded off his estate by buying the remains of the Rugmere Manor around Chalk Farm. In this same year, Charles Pratt, Baron **Camden,** who held property on the east side of the road to Hampstead, was made Earl Camden. He decided to create a small new town on his estate and Camden Town was started in 1790. Lord Southampton followed suit and granted building leases on the opposite side of the road, where rather humbler houses were erected.

By the start of the 19th century, London was advancing rapidly from the south. Regent's Park developed with the backing of the Prince Regent (later George IV) from 1811 onwards and with it the houses and markets on the Crown land to the east, while terraces continued up the Hampstead Road. The Regent's Canal started in this sector after 1812 and the Zoological Gardens were established in 1828. Lord Southampton and Eton

College began to think it was time to turn their fields into building plots. Tentative plans were prepared, but these had to be modified by the arrival of the London and Birmingham Railway in the 1830s.

In 1840, when the Eton Estate had already started building in a small way, the then Lord Southampton put his northerly property up for sale. A 3-day auction was held in August and his lands in Highgate, Kentish Town, northern Camden Town and Chalk Farm fetched together some £48,000 for the freeholds, at an average price of £300 per acre. Included in the sale were plots on the west side of the present Regent's Park Road on the lower slopes of Primrose Hill, and Eton also intended to build over its adjoining land on the Hill, but this was stopped by popular agitation, which had already succeeded in preventing the construction of a cemetery on these same slopes. The Crown accordingly bought Lord Southampton's plots,

including the site of St Mark's Church, for £2,194 and took the Eton property in exchange for some Crown land near the school. Primrose Hill was reserved as a park by an Act of Parliament of 1842.

Housing development then continued slowly but steadily over those parts of our area which had not become park, railway or canal. Many of the original buildings survive today, except where destroyed by bombing in the second World War, 1939-45 (WW II). This was particularly severe in the closely-packed terracing east of Regent's Park (section 1B). Other buildings have since fallen to the needs of traffic or the decay of age, but in general it is not difficult to envisage the area as it was 150 or more years ago.

Section 1 The Crown Estate in Camden

Camden's Nash Terraces
(see maps 1-2 at end of book)

14   *Gloucester Gate in 1827, showing the two lodges as originally built, linked by a severely classical screen*

THE STORY OF **REGENT'S PARK** begins in 1539 when the area was enclosed as a hunting ground for Henry VIII. The deer park was cut somewhat arbitrarily from the surrounding woods and fields, paying little heed to existing boundaries, so that although known as Marybone Park (variously spelt) its eastern side was in St Pancras.

The land was used as a reward for services rendered during and after the Civil War by both King Charles and Cromwell: the leaseholders asset-stripped for a quick profit and cut down the trees to sell. The Crown continued to lease the Park as farmland until 1790, when the Surveyor realised the potential of building development, and the final farm leases ended in 1811. The task of designing a new estate was entrusted to John Nash, already a favourite of the Prince Regent (later George IV), the keen supporter of the new park in whose honour it was named. Nash's vision was of an exclusive residential area for the well-to-do. Rejecting the grid pattern of earlier estates, his plan was based on two eccentric circles, lined with stuccoed terraces of palatial appearance. 56 villas would be dotted around the open parkland, which was flanked on the north by a landscaped extension of the Grand Union Canal, itself promoted by Nash.

Development began in earnest at the end of the Napoleonic Wars, and the Park as we know it was effectively complete by 1828. While public money was spent on the open spaces and roadways, building plots were assigned to private builders who developed them as commercial ventures, working to Nash's exterior designs. Fortunately for us, not all of Nash's original plans were realised – only 8 villas were built, and the north side of the Park was left undeveloped to preserve the 'beautiful' views northwards. Nor did the area remain exclusive for long: the Zoological Gardens arrived in 1828, and by mid-century most of the Park had been opened up for public recreation.

At the end of the second World War (WW II) in 1945 the buildings of the Park were in a sorry state – two-thirds of them empty, and few unaffected by bomb damage or general neglect. Though some favoured razing all to the ground and starting afresh, the Gorell Commission of 1946 recommended that the terraces be fully restored to give them another 60 years of useful life. Twelve years later the Crown Commissioners began restoration of the main terraces, which by the late 1970s was all but complete, preserving for us this 'unique national heritage'. Not only the Grade I-listed buildings delight the eye. Decorative iron railings abound, many sporting their maker's name and Grade II-listed in their own right; as do bollards and lamp-posts in 1820s style but bearing the insignias of various monarchs from George IV to Elizabeth II.

Our first walk begins at St Mark's Square, 100 yards east of the Zoo bus stop at the foot of Primrose Hill. We enter the Park by the attractive footbridge over the Regent's Canal. Narrow-boat berths to the left occupy the only remaining stump of the Collateral Cut, a branch of the canal which once ran south to the Cumberland Basin (p 27). The 'floating' Chinese restaurant is, in fact, built firmly on the canal bed!

Crossing the Outer Circle, follow the **BROAD WALK**, the modern Camden-Westminster boundary, which in winter offers fine views over the long sweep of Camden's Nash terraces to the east. At the top of the gentle slope is the **Parsee Drinking Fountain**, erected by the gift of Sir Cowasgee Gehangir Readymoney in 1869 as a token of gratitude for the protection enjoyed by the Parsees under the British Protectorate. While the Broad Walk continues south towards Park Square, we briefly retrace our steps and follow a path leading north-eastwards to a playground by the **OUTER CIRCLE**. Uneven ground on the right marks the site of St Katharine's Lodge, a villa designed c1828 by Ambrose Poynter as a residence for the Master of nearby St Katharine's (p 16). The lodge served during WW I as a hospital for officers, and later as part of the West London Hospital for Nervous

Diseases, before damage by a flying bomb in 1944 led to its demolition.

Ahead lies **GLOUCESTER GATE**, the original East Gate to the Park, named like most 'streets' on the estate after a royal duke (see panel). Nash's decorative screen of 1825-6, with its cast iron gates and Doric columns, was removed when the road was widened in 1878, and the two old lodges now stand side by side to the north of the road. To their east are a grotto and defunct **drinking fountain**, with a bronze statue by Joseph Durham of a milkmaid: water once sprang from the Cornish rock into her overflowing pail. **Nos.14** and **15** opposite, once private houses, have since 1950 played a largely educational role, home successively to the American School (now near Swiss Cottage); North Bridge House school (now at 1 Gloucester Avenue, p 81); and currently the **Prince of Wales' Institute of Architecture**, launched in 1992 to promote traditional architectural values. No.14 (once Gloucester House) adjoins **No.12**, whose Ionic façade faces the Park. Known originally as Strathirne Lodge, and later as Gloucester Lodge, it was built in c1826 for a diplomat brother of the Master of St Katharine's.

Set back from the Outer Circle, and still partly residential, **Nos.1-11** were erected by Richard Mott in 1827 as Gloucester Terrace. The last Nash terrace to be built in the Park, it has three Ionic porticoes,

and pediments at either end graced by female statues. The unusually large cornices were the work of J J Scoles, the builder's site architect, who disliked Nash's planned façade and cheekily tried to improve it by doubling their size: a bemused John Nash barely noticed the change. **A blue plaque at No.6** recalls the residence from 1920 until his death in 1936 of Sir Henry Wellcome, the American-born pharmaceuticals manufacturer and founder of the Wellcome Trust. The mews to the rear of this terrace, and of some others yet to come, open onto Albany Street, and will be viewed from there in section 1B.

Beyond Gloucester Gate, the buildings of **ST KATHARINE'S PRECINCT** were erected in 1828 to house the St Katharine's Foundation, displaced from its previous site near the Tower of London by the construction of St Katharine's Dock. Partly financed by the dock company, they included a chapel and school, flanked by residences for the members of the Foundation, elderly clergymen or their widows. The architect, Ambrose Poynter, was a pupil of Nash, but his gothic style contrasted with that of every other building in the Park. The western half of the twin-towered chapel is faced with Bath stone, while the other (Albany Street) end is plain brick. The walls facing the Outer Circle bear stone memorials to former patrons of the Foundation: Matilda (wife of King

Stephen) who founded it in 1147 to help the poor; Eleanor (wife of Henry III); and George IV. After wartime damage to the buildings, the Foundation moved in 1948 to Stepney, close to its original home.

The Family of George III

Sons:
George IV, PRINCE REGENT, **Prince of Wales**, Earl of CHESTER
Frederick, Bishop of Osnabruck (OSNABURGH), Duke of **York** & ALBANY
WILLIAM IV, Duke of CLARENCE, Duke of ST ANDREW'S, Earl of MUNSTER
Ernest, King of Hanover, Duke of CUMBERLAND
AUGUSTUS, Duke of Sussex
Adolphus, 1st Duke of CAMBRIDGE

Mary, one of three daughters, married William, Duke of GLOUCESTER

Derivations of local street names **past** and PRESENT are highlighted.

St Katharine's was then restored and transferred to the use of the Danish community in London. The **Danish Church**, as the chapel is now known, boasts 17th century wooden figures carved by Caius Cibber, and brought from the old Danish church at Limehouse. Surprisingly sited in the grounds is a brightly painted replica of the runic **Jelling Stone**. The original was set up at Jelling in Denmark by King Harald Bluetooth (reigned 940-985) to commemorate his parents and the conversion of his country to Christianity.

Next, behind a private communal garden, comes breath-taking **CUMBERLAND TERRACE** (1826). Over 800 feet long, it has seven Ionic porticoes, and comprises three main blocks linked by arches leading into small courtyards. The large pediment in the centre honours Britannia and the 'various arts, sciences, trades, etc., that mark her empire', a theme echoed in the terracotta statues adorning the skyline. The statuary by George Bubb may not be especially good, but Nash's aim was for overall effect. He was determined to impress since in the Park, facing the terrace, there was to have been a 'guinguette' or pleasure palace for the Prince Regent himself; this never materialised. In the early 1960s the terrace was completely reconstructed behind its Nash façade, the original 33 houses becoming 12 houses and 44 flats.

The novelist Elizabeth Gaskell stayed with friends at **No.17**, probably in 1859, while 30 years later, at **No.7**, lived Sir James Crichton Brown, a specialist in lunacy. **No.4** was home in 1910 to actress Dame Marie Tempest, while fellow thespian Gladys Cooper was at **No.18** in 1916, the year in which she first performed at the Playhouse Theatre. At the same

house in the 1920s lived H B Irving (elder son of Sir Henry Irving) and his actress wife Dorothea Baird, who created the part of Trilby in the play of that name by George du Maurier. The latter's son Gerald, another actor-manager, lived at **No.24** in 1907-16 before moving to Hampstead; his second daughter Daphne, the future novelist, was born here in 1907. More recent residents have been Lena Jeger, MP and former St Pancras councillor, television globetrotter Alan Whicker and the actor Sir Ralph Richardson.

CUMBERLAND PLACE, also of 1826, is a block of four houses in Corinthian style. Nash placed their entrance porches at the rear so that the front would appear like one large mansion. Behind is **CHESTER PLACE** (1825-26), a quiet backwater with its rear facing Albany Street. **No.10** was the home of Sara Coleridge, daughter of the poet Samuel, from 1837 until her death in 1852. She translated Latin and Greek, edited her father's work and wrote fairy tales. Sir Gerald du Maurier lived at **No.5** before moving to Cumberland Terrace. Ignaz Moscheles, pianist, composer and conductor, lived at **No.3** in 1830-46. His visitors included Liszt, Paganini and Felix Mendelssohn, whose *Elijah* was first rehearsed here in 1846. The following year Charles Dickens rented a house in the Place to be near his son Charley, who had

scarlet fever and was being nursed at the nearby home of the Hogarths, Dickens' in-laws. Charles and his wife Kate had abandoned a trip to Paris on hearing of Charley's illness, but were unable to return to their house in Devonshire Terrace as it had been let to tenants. Dickens' seventh child, Sydney, was born at Chester Place, while his father laboured on instalments of the serialised *Dombey and Son*.

Straight ahead are the modern flats and houses of **CHESTER CLOSE NORTH**, replacing the old mews area of **CHESTER TERRACE**, which we now veer right to inspect. It was built in 1825 by James Burton, second only to Nash in the amount he invested in the Park. Over 900 feet long, it has 3 Corinthian porticoes of 8 columns at each end and in the centre, with further 6-column porches in between. The longest terrace in the Park, it was also, when first built, the most troublesome. An otherwise preoccupied John Nash had failed to supervise the work which, when complete, was not to his taste. Statues by Bubb surmounting each of the terrace's 52 columns he described as 'ridiculous', ordering their removal. He disliked the pavilions at either end, which protruded in front of the terrace, spoiling its appearance: these, he demanded, should be demolished. Eventually the pavilions were reprieved, but the statues were removed to Cumberland Terrace. The triumphal arches at each end of the terrace were

18   *Centrepiece of Cumberland Terrace (T H Shepherd, 1827)*

added by Nash to soften the effect of the protruding blocks. Damaged in WW II, the terrace was restored in the 1960s, still as 42 individual houses. A **blue plaque** at **No.13** commemorates the architect C R Cockerell, who died here in 1863. North Villa, on which he collaborated with Decimus Burton, survives (though much altered) on the west side of the Park as the Islamic Cultural Centre. **No.31** was home in his later years to dramatist Alfred Sutro (1863-1933), best known for his translations of Maeterlinck. A later resident of the terrace was Michael Codron, the West End producer who helped launch the careers of playwrights from Pinter to Ayckbourn.

CHESTER GATE (1825-6), originally Cambridge Place, links the Outer Circle with Albany Street. In 1953-8 **No.5** was a pied à terre of Benjamin Britten, whose true home at the time was his beloved Aldeburgh. Overlooking the garden of **Nash House** (officially 3 Chester Terrace) is a bust of the architect copied from that by local sculptor William Behnes (p 31) and placed there by a 20th-century successor of the Duke of Wellington.

Leading off Chester Gate are **CAMBRIDGE TERRACE MEWS** which, unlike some neighbouring mews, have escaped redevelopment. Back on the Outer Circle is **CAMBRIDGE TERRACE**, twelve houses of simple design, reconstructed after wartime

damage as facsimiles of the originals, and now a mix of offices and flats. **No.10** is the headquarters of a cancer research funding organisation.

Statues representing the Three Graces adorn the entrances to French-styled **CAMBRIDGE GATE**. Dating only from 1876-80, this was built by Archer & Green as flats, its Bath stone contrasting with the stucco of its neighbours. A candidate for demolition after WW II, the terrace survived, and in 1994 complete renovation was imminent, the ballroom of **No.10** to become a swimming pool. An early resident of **No.8**, in 1887-99, was a young John Galsworthy, called to the Bar at Lincoln's Inn in 1890. Caryl Brahms, the theatre and ballet critic, occupied a flat at **No.3** in 1982, the year she died.

Cambridge Gate stands on the site of the Colosseum, designed by Decimus Burton (son of James) and opened in 1830. It housed a huge panorama of London, covering 40,000 sq ft of canvas, and derived from 2,000 drawings made by Thomas Hornor in a cabin on the dome of St Paul's. An alternative panorama of Paris by night was exhibited in the evenings in 1846. The unusual building was 16-sided and 130 feet in diameter, with a Doric portico and cupola. Its name related to its colossal size rather than to any similarity to its namesake in Rome: in fact it rather resembled the Pantheon. A hydraulic lift gave access to the upper galleries and roof,

from which the actual panorama could be seen, in company with the original ball and cross from St Paul's which had been replaced and brought here. Further attractions were added, such as marine caverns, a jungle with stuffed animals, and a concert hall opening onto Albany Street. Though popular at first, the Colosseum was not a financial success. Despite various changes in ownership, and increasingly down-market entertainment, it closed and was demolished in 1875.

ST ANDREW'S PLACE dates from 1823-6. On its north side is the **Royal College of Physicians of London**, a T-shaped building of 1964, designed by Sir Denys Lasdun, architect of the National Theatre. Opinions differ as to how happily or otherwise it blends into the neighbourhood. Its centrepiece is an oak-panelled room pre-dating the Great Fire of 1666, and brought here from the College's earlier premises in the City and later Pall Mall. The dark blue brick structure at the Outer Circle end houses a partly sunken lecture theatre, behind which is a garden with, appropriately, a Hippocratic plane tree raised in the Chelsea Physic Garden. An unlabelled bust (sculptor and date unknown) is believed to be of Thomas Linacre, the royal physician who founded the College in 1518. Removed from the College's previous location, the bust was discovered in the 1980s in a private garden. A **blue plaque** records the residence 'on this site' of Frank Buckland, medical naturalist (p 24).

The College occupies the site of the Adult Orphan Asylum, designed free of charge by Nash in 1824 as a home for orphaned daughters of clergymen and officers. The young ladies moved to Ealing in 1882, whereafter the building became a private residence, known successively as Cambridge, then Scudamore, and finally Someries House.

The Royal College has acquired and restored the whole of St Andrew's Place. At the far end **Nos.9** and **10**, with a splendid Corinthian porch, are now known as Hayward House in honour of the Hayward Foundation, which helped finance the restoration. Their 'back' doors form part of the Albany Street frontage (p 24). In 1986 the newly pedestrianised complex was opened by the Queen as St

20   *The Diorama before it was built into Park Square East*

Andrew's Medical Precinct. It houses the offices of various medical specialty societies.

The Outer Circle now turns westward, along the north side of Park Square, whose gardens and western terrace are in Westminster. We, however, continue southward along Camden's Ionic-pilastered **PARK SQUARE EAST** (1823-5), which was in the throes of renovation in 1994. At roof level above **No.18** an inscription recalls the original use of the premises below as the London Diorama. This illuminated picture show, a forerunner of the cinema, was brought from Paris in 1823 by Frenchman Louis Daguerre, later famous as a pioneer of photography, to be managed after 1830 by his associate Charles Marie Bouton. Behind the Nash façade is the polygonal rotunda which housed the spectacle, its original interior designed by Auguste C. Pugin, father of the better known Augustus Welby Pugin. Inside was a revolving auditorium, seating 200, from which two vast panoramas, part canvas and part transparency, could be viewed in turn, with ingenious lighting effects to make them appear alive. Typical scenes were of gothic ruins or churches by day and by night, Alpine valleys at various seasons of the year, and disasters such as landslides or volcanic eruptions. A roaring success at first, the Diorama eventually fell prey to competition from cheaper imitations, finally closing in 1851.

To see the rotunda, continue to the traffic lights at Marylebone Road, where two left turns lead into **PETO PLACE** (once Albany Mews). In 1848 the Diorama had been sold to Sir Samuel Morton Peto, builder, railway contractor and Baptist, who in 1852 converted the rotunda into the Regent's Park Baptist Chapel, adding external buttresses for a more churchy appearance, and replacing the glasshouse windows which had provided the natural lighting for the picture show. After closure of the chapel in 1922, the building served for 30 years as a rheumatism treatment pool of the Middlesex Hospital, and later as an annexe of Bedford College. From 1980 to 1993 it was the home of a co-operative devoted to disability arts and art therapy, now exiled to Osnaburgh Street (p 31) but retaining its name of Diorama Arts. Schemes to demolish the rotunda and to convert it into an arts centre, mosque or car park all foundered: in 1994 it was being weather-proofed, its future still uncertain.

Peto Place bisects **Albany Terrace** (1823-5), effectively two blocks facing Marylebone Road. The ornate lamps outside **No.2**, adorned by tiny gryphons, are Grade II-listed. The building, by an unknown architect, was restored in 1988 as offices for the Consumers' Association. Its extension along Albany Street is a sympathetic pastiche, betrayed by the modern windows and pristine brickwork to the rear. It stands on the site of a Victorian repository known as the Albany Pantechnicon, which later became Dunlop House and served the rubber company for several decades.

Here, on the threshold of the very different area described in the next section, this walk ends. Great Portland Street station is adjacent, Warren Street station some 400 yards eastward along the Euston Road.

22   *Houses in Park Village East seen from Cumberland Basin (T H Shepherd, 1827) (see p 27)*

Nash's service area and the Park Villages

(see map 2 at end of book)

THE CROWN LAND between Regent's Park and Augustus Street was set aside by Nash as a service area of markets, shops and decent working-class housing. Three markets were planned, to serve which the Collateral Cut of the canal approached from the north, opening out into Cumberland Basin. To the north Nash found room for the cavalry barracks, and beyond them he created the pretty Park Villages, forerunner of many later 'garden suburbs'. Begun in 1811, development of the area was slow, taking over two decades to complete.

In the service area proper, the street plan was devised by Nash, but very few of the buildings were of his design. Of the three proposed markets only one materialised, the sites intended for the others being laid out as residential squares. Booth's poverty map of 1889 shows Albany Street as a great divide between the opulence of the Park and the workaday world of the service area. Whereas the Outer Circle was classed as wealthy, and Albany Street as middle-class, the streets to the east were 'fairly comfortable', with small pockets of poverty: as early as 1831 Nash had

received complaints that intended stables were being turned into human habitations. Small factories eventually appeared in narrow strips of land along the eastern border of the estate.

The 20th-century transformation of the district began around 1930, when the Crown Estate flats were built around the then disused Basin. Much of the area was devastated by bombing in WW II, and afterwards lay derelict. In 1951 32 acres of land were sold by the Crown to St Pancras Borough Council for redevelopment as part of the modern Regent's Park Estate, built to house some 1700 families. Among its several architects was Sir Frederick Gibberd, noted inter alia for his work on Harlow New Town.

This walk begins where the last section ended, at the south end of **ALBANY STREET**. Roadworks began here in 1811, roughly on the line of a track running north from Coneyburrow Farm, whose name suggests a profusion of rabbits at some time, and whose buildings were on the site of **Holy Trinity**. Built by Sir John Soane in 1827-9, and closed in 1952, the church is now the headquarters of the

**Some Albany Street Residents
c1830 - c1850**
(Post - 1864 house numbering scheme)

THOMAS SHOTTER BOYS, painter of continental cityscapes, nos.36 & 48

SAMUEL COUSINS, mezzotint engraver, no.13: see also pp.31 & 52

AUGUST W. HOFMANN, German chemist, no.52: see CHR 18

CHARLES HORN, singer, composer of the song Cherry Ripe, no.44

Sir WILLIAM JENNER, physician, expert on typhus & typhoid, nos.24 & 16

HENRY JOHNSON, watercolorist, no.61

FREDERICK LABLACHE, opera singer who appeared with Jenny Lind, nos.42, 51

RICHARD MOTT, builder of several Nash terraces, no.75

THOMAS OLIPHANT, composer and madrigal collector, no.66

RAMSAY R. REINAGLE, portrait and animal painter, no.58

JOHN THELWALL, elocutionist and reformer, no.54: see DNB

JAMES VETCH, engineer and Conservator of UK Harbours, no.39

ABRAHAM WIVELL, portrait painter and fire safety activist, no.62

BENJAMIN D. WYATT, architect, son of James; designer of Drury Lane Theatre and Duke of York's Column, no.43

SPCK. The boundary between St Pancras and St Marylebone used to pass through the site, but was adjusted to include the whole of the church in the latter parish: it is thus outside the scope of this book.

North of Holy Trinity, and covering the site of Frederick Mews (once a preserve of horse cab owners), is the 9-storey, star-shaped block known as the **White House**. Built in 1936 by Robert Atkinson as self-contained service apartments, it was converted in 1975 into a 600-bed hotel, though one wing is still leased separately as flats. Reliefs on either side depict nude boys with various arcadian motifs.

On the corner of Longford Street is the **Queen's Head and Artichoke** public house. The origin of its name is uncertain, having been attributed both to Elizabeth I's gardener and to Daniel Clarke, master cook to Elizabeth and James I, who held the lease of Tottenhall Manor. Dating from the 16th century and once, maybe, a royal hunting lodge, it appeared in Crew's survey of 1753 as a ramshackle old tavern. It was rebuilt on its present site in 1811, but the existing building dates only from c1900. Next door at **No.34** Albany Street, with an elaborate roofed balcony, is the oldest house on the estate, built in 1812.

The west side of the road is lined for much of its length by the rear elevations or mews areas of sites on the Outer Circle described in section 1A. **Nos.31** and **33**, with their Corinthian porch and urn, are

the 'back' entrances to 9-10 St Andrew's Place (p 20). The middle-class terraces of Albany Street attracted residents from many professional and artistic walks of life (see panel) but only some of their houses survive. The grey brick east face of the Royal College of Physicians covers the site of No.37, home from 1865 until his death in 1880 of Francis Trevelyan Buckland, commemorated by a plaque in the College garden. Trained as a surgeon, he later became an authority on fish, and kept exotic pets such as bears and monkeys, which were said to run loose in his house.

The red brick flats of **Colosseum Terrace** (1878), stuccoed at ground floor level, replaced the concert hall of the erstwhile Colosseum. An archway leads into **CAMBRIDGE GATE MEWS**, redevelopment of which was imminent in 1994. Back in Albany Street, **No.55** bears a **blue plaque** recalling Henry Mayhew, author of *London Labour and the London Poor* and founder of *Punch,* who lived here in the 1840s. The architect Robert Edis was resident at the same address in 1864-6 (see Edis Street, p 79). In 1851 organ builder Henry Willis, whose creations include the instruments in Alexandra Palace and St Paul's, opened a workshop at **No.75**. This house and some of its neighbours once had wooden shop fronts of which there is now no trace.

On the east side of the street, the 1960s **police station**, with a traditional blue

lamp, replaced an earlier establishment further north. Though rebuilt since WW II, the **Cape of Good Hope** has quenched local thirsts since the street's earliest days. Its predecessor still stood in 1949 at the corner of William Street, which then ran through to here from Hampstead Road. Tucked away behind the pub is **St Bede's Hall**, an island of Victorian gothic in a sea of modernity. It opened in 1877 as a mission hall, part of Christ Church (p 25). After closure at the time of WW I, it was used as a clubroom by both St James's and St Mary Magdalene. Later a judo club, and now a health and fitness centre, its present-day patrons fight the flab rather than the devil. On the OS map of 1894 St Bede's is shown as an RC Chapel, but this was a mistake. A Catholic convent school was, in fact, sited immediately to the north. Known as St Ann's [sic], it was founded in 1853 and run for some 65 years by the Order of the Holy Child. From 1857 its chapel served as a mission church, Queen of Martyrs and St Pancras, until replaced in 1938 by St Anne's (p 36).

North of St Bede's, and now only a service road, is part of **LITTLE ALBANY STREET**, which once ran parallel to its parent street between Longford Street and the Victory pub. It was the scene of a rat-catching anecdote in Book 3 of Mayhew's *London Labour.* Back in Albany Street, **Troutbeck** is a long block of council flats with basement level workshops and, like most nearby council blocks, a Lake District name (see panel, p 32).

A betting shop at the junction with Robert Street occupies the site of No.124, home in 1831-2 to young Edward Lear and his older sister. Albany Street was a step up from their previous rooms off Gray's Inn Road, and more convenient for the Zoo, where Lear had made the drawings for his book *The Family of Parrots*, and where he still worked as a freelance draughtsman. Beyond **Windermere** is the **Victory** pub, rebuilt in modern style on its original site, though the stone of its boundary wall appears much older. Commemorating the architect of the Park is **NASH STREET**, an L-shaped service road which absorbed former Cumberland Street and the north end of Little Albany Street.

On the west side of Albany Street, at the corner of Chester Gate, the restored **Chester Arms** pub has a 20th-century front on the ground floor. Behind a wall the modern flats and houses of **CHESTER CLOSE SOUTH** occupy part of the old mews area of Chester Terrace. **Chester Court** is a block of flats with a row of shops beneath (a reminder that this part of the street was once its shopping centre) – a long, mainly 4-storey, terrace in dark brick. Between 1830 and 1850 several notable artists had addresses here (see panel, p 26).

Rothay flats opposite replaced a building with a fascinating history. Designed free of charge by Nash, it opened in 1818 as an ophthalmic hospital for soldiers who had served in the Egyptian campaigns (p 10). By 1821 it had become a workshop of Sir Goldsworthy Gurney, celebrated for the steam carriage which he built here and drove to Bath and back at an average speed of 15 mph. Steam guns, an early and unsuccessful form of machine gun, were made here in the early 1830s by Perkins & Bacon. In 1835 Sir Felix Booth, of London Gin fame, took a lease on the building which, partly rebuilt, later became a brandy distillery and vinegar brewery of Grimble & Co. Around 1900 it was a base of both the General Omnibus Co. and the rival Vanguard Motorbus Co. Bombed in WW II, the building was demolished in 1967.

To the north is former Christ Church (1837), first fruit of Bishop Blomfield's Church Extension Scheme. Designed in the classical style by Sir James Pennethorne, with furnishings by Butterfield, it has a huge door and a slim spire above. A window depicting the Sermon on the Mount was executed by William Morris from a design by Dante Gabriel Rossetti. The latter's mother and sisters worshipped here for many years, attracted by the High Church ritual: they may have heard sermons by Manning, Keble or Pusey of the Oxford Movement, all of whom preached here. Christ Church closed in 1989, its parish merging with that of St Mary Magdalene (p 30), but the building has a new lease of life as the Greek Orthodox **St George's Cathedral**.

No.166, on the school playground site, was 45 Upper Albany Street until 1864, when the two halves of the street were integrated and renumbered. Here was the home from 1854 to 1867 of the Rossetti family, and here was written Christina's best-known poem, *Goblin Market*. Her brother Dante Gabriel meanwhile led a Bohemian life elsewhere in London, visiting occasionally.

Across the road is the rear elevation of Chester Place, where the **Prince George of Cumberland** (c1825) stood vacant and 'to let' in 1994. Since the King's brother Ernest was Duke of Cumberland when the pub was built, the dedication must be either to another duke, or a mistake. Beyond lie **CUMBERLAND TERRACE MEWS**, the southern part replaced by modern flats and houses, the northern half largely unchanged. Albany Street's double granite **horse trough**, erected in 1882 by the Metropolitan Drinking Fountain Association, was probably the gift of Mr *Clement* Upton-Cottrell-Dormer of Rousham House (Oxon) and Berkeley Square, whose wife was named *Florence* – hence the enigmatic inscriptions.

Opposite are the utilitarian **Regent's Park Barracks**, built in 1820-21 for the Life Guards, complete with hospital and chapel. They housed generations of soldiers ready for ceremonial duty in the capital, besides being a Territorial Army base after WW II (as a faded legend testifies), and latterly accommodating the Army's transport squadron. In 1993 the MOD began redevelopment of parts of the

---

More Albany Street Occupants

Troutbeck site

LUIGI ARDITI, composer and conductor, no.82, 1869-87
HENRY DIXON, photographer; his shop was at no.112: see p.61 & CHR 9, p.17
JOHN FRANCIS, sculptor; made busts of Victoria and Albert, no.112, 1834-61

Windermere site

MICHAEL COSTA, composer-conductor, future Director of the Italian Opera, no.144, 1840-46

Chester Court stretch

GEORGE FRIPP, painter of Balmoral
BENJAMIN GIBBON, line engraver of works by Landseer
E.T. PARRIS, painter of the Colosseum panorama; inventor of a paint ingredient called Parris's Medium
JOHN LAPORTE, watercolorist, and his son GEORGE, animal painter to the King of Hanover
JAMES THOMSON, engraver

---

site 'in the national interest', despite strong local opposition. Over the road the occasional Bubb statue may be glimpsed, perched incongruously above the back of Cumberland Terrace, which is as drab as its front is spectacular: Nash's concern was for the view of his terraces from the Park. Beyond the rear of St Katharine's, **No.197** was home in 1869-72 to E W Godwin, both an architect and a costume designer for Liberty's store. Constant Lambert, the conductor and composer, lived there too for 3 years before his death in 1951.

The **Park Villages** (1823-34) were developed by Nash very much as a hobby in the years before his retirement, and completed by his stepson and pupil James Pennethorne. The cottages are a riot of different styles – some classical or Italianate, others Gothic or Tudor. Their variety of design was to be a model for many suburban estates before WW II.

PARK VILLAGE WEST, on a triangular site between Albany Street and the abandoned canal, begins at **Nos.1-7** with a terrace of miniature houses by Pennethorne. The village was once reputedly home to ladies of easy virtue, and is so portrayed, under the fictional name of Florizel, in Michael Sadleir's novel *Fanny by Gaslight*. Known residents were more respectable! Tudor-Gothic **No.17** bears a **blue plaque** recording the foundation by Dr Pusey in 1845 of 'the first religious sisterhood in the Church of

England since the Reformation'. Named the Order of the Holy Cross, it later moved to Osnaburgh Street (p 31). At **No.8** lived James Wyld, geographer to Queen Victoria, who in 1851 displayed in Leicester Square a gigantic model of the earth 60 ft in diameter. **No.12**, the Italianate **Tower House**, has an octagonal turret designed to be viewed from two directions. It was home to Dr James Johnson, physician to both Nash and William IV, and from 1848-52 to W P Frith, painter of *Derby Day at Paddington Station*. More recent occupants have been, successively, Woodrow Wyatt MP and royal dress designer Norman Hartnell. **Nos.15** and **16** were rebuilt as pastiches after wartime bomb damage. The Thomas Hardy resident in the village in 1863 was not the future Wessex novelist – then working nearby as Clerk of Works to the Midland Railway as it cut through the graves of St Pancras Churchyard – but Thomas Duffus Hardy, a future Keeper of the Public Record Office.

Back in Albany Street, **No.204** (Pennethorne House) is a modern development for the Humanist Housing Association. Opposite Nash's **Clarence Cottage** with its recumbent stone lion are his **Albany Lodge** and **GLOUCESTER GATE MEWS**, where Arthur Benjamin, pianist and composer, lived at **No.3** in 1950.

Turning right, we cross **Gloucester**

Gate Bridge over the former canal spur, stagnant by 1942 and filled in with wartime rubble: the Zoo car park beyond the bridge sits on the landfill. Since soil from the excavation of the canal was used to make bricks for building the Barracks and nearby streets, some of the earth may have come full circle! Replacing the earlier (1814) structure, the present bridge has a parapet which is part stone and part iron, but all to the same pattern. Stones record the building and opening of the new bridge in 1877-8, while a relief by C E Fucigna commemorates the death of St Pancras, the boy martyr beheaded under Diocletian in 304 AD – though the plaque shows him attacked by a wild beast.

A further right turn leads into **PARK VILLAGE EAST**, lined by 15 graceful St Pancras lamp-posts. Now a film studio, **No.1** was built, probably in the 1890s, in the garden of the York & Albany pub, and for over 30 years was a riding school. The rising line of windows facing the road is evidence of an internal ramp for its earlier equine occupants. The **horse statue** is reportedly a replica of the one which once adorned the riding school: its white-painted twin visible in the grounds of **No.6** is thought to be the original. The other houses on the east side of the village were swept away in 1900-06 when the railway was widened, but several Nash creations of c1824 still line the west side, their gardens sloping down to the level of

the old canal spur: most were built in pairs to simulate a single mansion (see pp 22,28). The first house, **Penrhyn Lodge**, has attractive stained glass and trellis work. The Fabian Sidney Webb was at Tudor-Gothic **No.4** in 1889, and Charlotte Haldane (p 78) at **No.16** in 1934. The stone lion here is obvious, but don't miss another feline eyeing the railway from the roof of the north wing. The next pair of houses was bombed in WW II and replaced by the modern **Nash House**. Further south, railway carriage sheds now lie where large villas were once scattered along Serpentine Road, while Crown Estate flats have replaced some villas between the railway and canal spur. **Silsoe House**, winner of the Worshipful Company of Tylers' Brickwork Award in 1972, is followed by **Richmond House**, a classical pastiche built in 1961 on the site of Augustus Square.

Goldsmith House, which is a YWCA hostel, and **Tintern House**, a 1930s block of Crown flats, stand at the junction with **AUGUSTUS STREET**, into which we turn. Its east side, following the Crown Estate boundary, and now bordered by post-WW II blocks, was once a pleasing terrace of stuccoed workers' cottages dating from 1819-26. At No.31 George Cruikshank, illustrator of Dickens, caricaturist and temperance reformer, kept a second home for his mistress Adelaide Archbold and their large family, while

living with his childless, and blissfully ignorant, wife at 263 Hampstead Road (p 41). To the west of the street was another Nash enterprise, the Cumberland (or Regent's Park) Basin at the southern end of the Collateral Cut, completed in 1818. Intended to handle farm produce from rural Middlesex, the Basin dealt also with ice, coal and timber, as well as stone and marble for monumental masons in the Euston Road. Factories were eventually built on the eastern side, where here in Augustus Street modern blocks of council flats now occupy a pocket of Camden-owned land.

Beyond them is **Datchet House** (1930-31), opened by the then Prince of Wales (later Edward VIII), the first block in the **Cumberland Market Estate**. Begun under the surveyorship of architect C E Varndell, this Crown Estate development of affordable housing comprises ten massive blocks in stock brick, built on three sides of the Basin site. Turn right along the north side of Cumberland Market, where the imposing clock tower of **Windsor House** overlooks a formal garden. Around the next corner in Redhill Street wharves and warehouses have given way to **Ascot House**, boasting an internal courtyard with ornamental fountain, and a bow-fronted **general store** facing the street; **Bagshot House**, with its ornamental urns; colonnaded **Swinley House** behind; and finally **Camberley**

Houses in Park Village East seen from the road (the 'York and Albany' to the right) (cf. p 22)

House (1937). Through gaps may be glimpsed the site of the old Basin, filled in and laid out as **allotments** still in use today, as well as the new lift shafts with pointed roofs added during a major refurbishment of the estate begun in the mid-1980s.

Cobbled **REDHILL STREET** was Edward Street until renamed by the Vestry in 1865 to avoid confusion with a nearby namesake (now Varndell Street, p 40); the vestrymen's choice of street names could be somewhat random. On its northern spur the flats of **Gardner House** (1963) recall the local Crown Estate surveyor in the 1950s. Pavement **bollards** in the service area have kept the same design since the time of Nash, the one here showing allegiance to Elizabeth II. Opposite is a mixed commercial and residential development of the early 1990s, comprising **Albany House** and **EDWARD MEWS**, once the top end of **LITTLE EDWARD STREET**, which retained its original name but survives only as a cul-de-sac behind the church.

Returning south down Redhill Street, we pass **Christ Church CE Primary School**, whose present building dates only from 1961, though its predecessor, on the Albany Street frontage, was listed as a National (ie Anglican) School in the 1842 Directory. The gothic building beyond bears an inscription stating that it was built on land granted by Queen Victoria: now

used as studios, it was once the boys' department of the school. Next comes a red brick building, built in 1912 as a garage for Vinot Cars, later a naval transport depot, and now housing a fashion company. It stands on the site of the Jew's Harp pub, once a rustic tavern with picturesque tea gardens in Marylebone Park, and relocated here when the Park was developed.

Beyond the **Dick Collins Hall** of the Regent's Park Residents' Association (named after Camden's Mayor of 1973), we regain **CUMBERLAND MARKET**. This was laid out in 1819 to house the hay and straw merchants of the Hay Market south of Piccadilly Circus, who moved here only in 1830. Beneath the west side was an enormous commercial ice well, 82 feet deep, owned by Robert Leftwich (also p 55). To keep local wells supplied, a ship sailed continuously between Norway and the Thames at Limehouse, where ice was transferred to canal barges. An annual rag fair was held in the square to coincide with the Hospital Rag Carnival, but the market itself was never a great success and closed in 1926, the ice well being filled in the 1930s with spoil from the Piccadilly Line extension to Cockfosters.

The market site remains an open space thanks to an 1830 Act of Parliament which forbade building on it. When in 1953 a community play centre was established here, a pensioned-off steam roller was left

behind as a giant toy. Later deemed dangerous, it was covered up with soil, to be rediscovered in 1989: it is being restored for use at local events. In 1965 the play centre was transformed into a unique, fully staffed children's paradise – a miniature town including a row of shops, and a road system with cars and traffic lights, an underpass and filling station. 'Traffic Town' amused local children until controversially closed in 1986. The now quiet open space is happily enlivened by the neighbourhood festival held here each summer, while the **Haymarket Centre** on the east side is a day-care facility for the elderly.

Until WW II the whole area from here southwards to Munster Square comprised terraces of working-class houses, mostly of 3 storeys, many with shops, coffee rooms or pubs on the ground floor. After extensive wartime damage to the area, all were demolished to make way for the modern Regent's Park Estate, with its low-rise blocks overlooked by loftier neighbours of 11 storeys or more. **Thirlmere**, on the west side of Cumberland Market, covers the site of No.49, once the studio of artist Robert Bevan, a member of the Camden Town Group. Here, every Saturday in 1914, he and fellow painters Ginner and Gilman put their work on public display, styling themselves the Cumberland Market Group. On the south side of the market a plaque recalls a visit to the estate in 1955 by the Duke of Edinburgh, while bollards honour George IV.

The roadway between **Grasmere** and **Patterdale** is officially a detached part of Osnaburgh Street, which once ran through

to here from the Euston Road. Follow it southwards to **ROBERT STREET**, whose eastern part is described in section 2. The later built western end was once named Ernest Street: whereas the Park terraces and local squares took the titles of George III's family, the humbler streets used their forenames (see panel, p 16). Redeveloped Robert Street embraces **COMPTON CLOSE**, over the road on the right, a community focal point with shops and a Camden **branch library**.

Continue straight ahead, beneath the flats opposite, into the area of the two markets which never materialised, now a partly cobbled, largely pedestrianised zone. Intended as a vegetable market,

CLARENCE GARDENS was instead developed in 1824 as a residential square. W H Davies, poet and 'super-tramp', lodged at No.2A before WW I. A pathway leads through the open space, once used as a nursery garden, but, like Munster Square beyond, opened for public use by the LCC in 1907 on a shilling (5p) lease from the Crown. Triumphantly relaid in 1972, the gardens have now had to be locked against vandals.

Ahead loom all 19 storeys of **The Combe**, passing either side of which will lead to **MUNSTER SQUARE** (1812-23), the meat market that never was. Before WW II, during which barrage balloons were reportedly stationed here, it was always regarded as a pleasantly spacious square. Leading anonymously off the south-east corner, diminutive **WYBERT STREET** is now but a garage access road – why *Wybert* nobody knows.

South of the square is **St Mary Magdalene** (1852), founded by the Rev Edward Stuart, a curate of Christ Church, whose aim was to create a church 'as near perfection' as humanly possible. Designed by Richard Carpenter as part of the Gothic Revival, the towerless building emphasised the chancel rather than the pulpit as the centre of worship. The east window of the north aisle is by A Welby Pugin. On the closure of Christ Church in 1989, the parishes of mother and daughter churches were reunited. **Clergy House** (of 1894),

on the corner of Longford Street, served as a presbytery until 1986, later being occupied by squatters. The church **school** (of 1901) was built next door in the Arts and Crafts style, with some fine Art Nouveau ironwork: it closed in 1970 and was later half demolished. In 1994 plans were in hand to refurbish Clergy House as flats, erect further apartments behind the school's listed façade, and build a new presbytery beyond. On the opposite corner of **LAXTON PLACE** is **St Anne's RC Church**, with a pleasing circular design in grey brick. Built on the site of a public house, it dates from 1970 when the congregation moved from Seaton Place (p 36). George Laxton was a baker of Cursitor Street (Chancery Lane) who bought properties locally in 1806.

LONGFORD STREET was one of several Frederick Streets until renamed in 1865 after a place near Windsor. At its western end, **Esther Randall Court**, a 1993 block of sheltered housing, is serviced by a short stump of Little Albany Street, beyond which stands Edwardian **Walton House**. The White House opposite (p 24) fronts onto **OSNABURGH TERRACE**, long bereft of its original houses. In 1844 Charles Dickens took lodgings at erstwhile No.9, leaving his children there, in the care of his brother Fred, while he and his wife toured America.

OSNABURGH STREET now extends only to Longford Street and none of its terraces survive. On the White House site, at No.21 (then No.26), composer Hector Berlioz spent two months in 1848, after eviction by bailiffs from the home of an opera promoter with whom he had been staying, and who had gone bankrupt.

A **blue plaque** recalls the foundation of the Fabian Society at No.17. Here was the flat of spiritualist Edward Pease, the society's first secretary: other founder members included H G Wells, the Webbs, and George Bernard Shaw.

From 1882 the young Shaw, then an unsuccessful novelist, lived opposite with his mother in second-floor rooms at No.36, a 'highly respectable house', he wrote. In 1887 the bankruptcy of the landlord forced the couple's hurried removal to Fitzroy Square. The bygone terrace on this east side of the street was home to several notable 19th-century artists (see panel). A succession of sculptors occupied No.30 (once No.10): William Behnes, whose work appears in St Paul's, followed by J H Foley and, from 1877, by his pupil Thomas Brock (also p86), whose studio and occasional home for over 40 years still stands behind modern **No.30**.

Pre-WW II industrial buildings now line the street, serving various commercial purposes. They include Goodyear House on the corner, built for the tyre company, and Strode House, erected for a long-established firm of gasfitters. **No.34**, a former cabinet factory, is now occupied by Diorama Arts (p 21). Beyond are two blocks of 1930s red brick mansion flats, linked by a grand archway leading only to a garage. **Marlborough House** bears a **blue plaque** erected in 1994 by the Dead Comics Society in memory of comic actor Kenneth Williams who lived here from 1972 until his death in 1988.

Opposite Holy Trinity is the site of St Saviour's Hospital, opened as a girls' orphanage in 1852 by the Park Village sisterhood (p 26). Their gothic chapel, designed free of charge by Butterfield, was later noted for its finely carved furnishings bought from a Carthusian church in Germany. In 1877 the sisterhood merged with the Devonport Sisters of Mercy, and the building was sold, to serve subsequently under various (mainly religious) auspices as a cancer hospital and later as a hospital for 'ladies of limited means'. It was closed in 1963 and demolished to make way for **Jellicoe House**. The **French Dispensary** on the ground floor relocated here c1970 from the now derelict Hôpital Français in Monmouth Street, Seven Dials.

And so we arrive at the Euston Road, close to our starting point, and only a short walk from Warren Street station where section 2 begins.

Some Residents of Osnaburgh Street
(Post-1876 house numbering scheme)

KENNY BAKER, jazz trumpeter, Regency House, c1950
KITTY CLAIRMONT, no.21, visited here by Heinrich Heine in 1827
CLAIRE CLAIRMONT, mistress of Lord Byron, mother of his child Allegra, no.21, 1847
HENRY COUSINS, engraver, no.40, 1830s-1860s; and his brother SAMUEL in the 1840s
JAMES HOLLAND, painter, no.32, c1856
JOHN SKINNER PROUT, painter, no.34, 1854
MARIO RAGGI, sculptor, no.44, c1880-c1900

Osnaburgh Terrace

ROBERT SMIRKE, RA, father of Sir Robert Smirke, designer of the British Museum

Some Block Names, Albany Street to Hampstead Road

Lake District & Cumbrian names

In Albany Street:
  Rothay, Troutbeck, Windermere
In Augustus Street
  Ambleside, Buttermere, Kendal
In Cumberland Market:
  Grisedale, Mosedale, Thirlmere, Wasdale
In Hampstead Road:
  Cartmel, Gillfoot, Rydal Water, Silverdale
In Harrington Square:
  Dalehead, Hurdwick House, Oxenholme
In Harrington Street:
  Ainsdale, Coniston, Kirkstone, Newlands
In Osnaburgh Street [northern section]:
  Grasmere, Patterdale
In Robert Street:
  Borrowdale, Derwent, Newby
In Stanhope Street:
  Eskdale, Hawkshead, Langdale, Scafell
In Varndell Street:
  Ennerdale, Staveley, The Tarns,
  Waterhead

Berkshire names

In Albany Street: Tilehurst
In Clarence Gardens: Englefield
In Munster Square:
  (The) Combe, Marlston, Swallowfield
In Stanhope Street: Bucklebury,
  Pangbourne
cf Compton Close - after a Berks. village

Maritime names

In Euston Centre, after admirals:
  Drummond Street: Beatty House
  Osnaburgh Street: Jellicoe House
cf Triton Square - after a Greek sea god

Section 2 East of the Crown Estate

(see map 2 at end of book)

Invented & Painted by Wm Hogarth.

.A REPRESENTATION of the MARCH of the GUARDS towards SCOTLAND, in the YEAR 1745.

THE STRIP OF LAND some 300 yards wide between the Crown Estate and the Hampstead Road, which runs north from the Euston Road to Harrington Square, lies totally within the former Southampton Estate of the Fitzroy family. On the map of 1804 the Crown Estate to the west of the area was still farmland; building existed only along the New (now Euston) Road and in ribbon development up the west side of Hampstead Road about half-way to Camden Town. By 1827 these houses had reached Camden Town but, on the east side, development was completed more slowly, the frontage being punctuated by a reservoir and then St James's Chapel and Rhodes's farm. By 1890 the area was a mixed residential one with many small factories, but it was redeveloped with high-density housing (mostly multi-storey flats) after 1945. A very few of the original, mostly 19th-century, buildings survive. At the southern end the Euston Centre site was developed from the late 1960s as prestige office and commercial space, dominated by the 33-storey Euston Tower, nearly 400 feet tall, near the SW corner of Hampstead Road.

Engraving of Hogarth's painting
The March to Finchley (1750), owned
by the Thomas Coram Foundation

We start from Warren Street Underground station, at the junction of Tottenham Court Road and **EUSTON ROAD**, the latter renamed in 1857 after the Fitzroy family Suffolk estate. This is a major traffic artery started in the 1750s as a London bypass, the 'New Road' from Paddington to Islington on which live cattle could be driven to Smithfield Market without passing through residential or commercial areas, and also for the movement of troops. Its original line is now the two-lane westbound half of the road. The stipulation in the authorising Act of Parliament (1756) that no buildings were to be erected within 50 feet of the new road resulted in a series of long gardens, which later came to be used as stonemasons' and timber yards, the houses themselves being approached by a service road (here, Warren Street) to the south. The gardens or yards on the southern side of the Euston Road remained until about 1860, but they were soon to be built on. Several of the modest buildings erected still exist (eg **Nos.327-337**), behind which can be seen the tidy backs of some of the original Warren Street houses.

The first Underground Railway was built, by the cut and cover method, under the carriageway of the original Euston Road, and opened in 1863. The present Circle and Metropolitan Lines from Great Portland Street to Euston Square run just beneath the road surface. The much

deeper **Warren Street station** (opened 1907) is, however, on the Northern Line which runs up through Mornington Crescent, Camden Town and Chalk Farm - all stations mentioned in this survey. The station's striking 1930s stone façade is by Charles Holden, architect of nearby University of London Senate House in Malet Street (the façades of the other Northern Line stations were designed by Leslie Green, 1907).

Cross to the bottom of Hampstead Road. Before Euston Road was widened and the underpass built, there were two pubs on the NW and NE corners of this busy crossroads: the 'Adam and Eve' and the 'King's Head'. Both are shown in Hogarth's *The March to Finchley* of 1750. The painting (see *Camden History Review 3*) shows the Tottenham Court Turnpike, at the time of the 1745 Jacobite Rebellion, with the Grenadier Guards setting off northwards, in some disarray, to deal with Bonnie Prince Charlie. Hogarth's viewpoint of 250 years ago was what is now the middle of Tottenham Court Road. The Adam and Eve had gardens and entertainments in days when it could be the goal of a short walk into the country. Behind the King's Head was once the old manor of Tottenhall, whence comes the name of Tottenham Court.

The extent to which the **Euston Centre** complex has been built over the old network of roads is shown in the sketch-map. The fronts of the new buildings, including that of Euston Tower, coincide with the line of the former Eden Street which had been built on the gardens of the Adam & Eve. On the present Euston Road frontage the 20-storey Hodder Headliner building at **No.338** was originally (1967) built as the Rank Xerox building.

The first road to the left (west) off Hampstead Road is **DRUMMOND STREET**, the south side of which has been gobbled up by the Euston Centre development. It leads to the last part of the site still under development, namely **TRITON SQUARE**, where the Church of St Anne's (p 30) on Seaton Place was demolished in 1970, as was the 1870 London School Board building in the late 1980s.

From the northeast corner of Triton Square runs **STANHOPE STREET**, named in 1868 after William Stanhope, second Earl of Harrington, who married Catherine Fitzroy in 1746. It developed in three sections, firstly the part south of Drummond Street (now the east side of Triton Square) which was, from before 1793, Brook Street, named after a Mr Brook or Brooke who exhibited wild animals on the west side, close to the New Road. The Brook menagerie was in place by 1722. In 1841 Dickens called a Mr Herring of the New Road to attend to his sick raven. In 1904 the Street Directory records a William Herring still running a menagerie at 328 Euston Road. Next to the north is the stretch from Drummond Street to Varndell Street (Mary Street from 1804) and finally the original Stanhope Street, which from 1830 had continued northwards from Varndell Street. The three sections were integrated and renumbered as Stanhope Street in 1868.

In the 19th and early 20th centuries this whole area contained many small businesses, mostly in furniture and piano manufacturing, and in 1904 the Directory recorded in the immediate locality such trades as veneer merchants, japanners, wood carvers, wood turners, cabinet makers, upholsterers, looking-glass makers, glass bevellers, glass frame manufacturers and fret cutters. As a residential as well as an industrial area it also had its full share of bakers, fried fish and eel pie shops, coffee houses, dining rooms and public houses, while a cow keeper was still listed in 1904 on the corner of Stanhope Street and William Road.

The large companies housed in the Euston Centre have included Capital

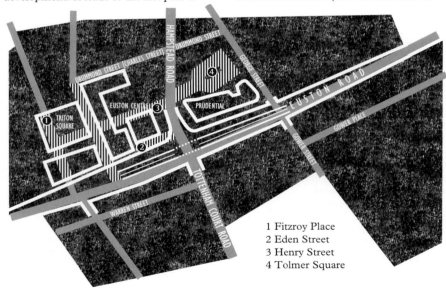

1 Fitzroy Place
2 Eden Street
3 Henry Street
4 Tolmer Square

Effect of Euston Road widening and development (1960s)

Radio and, until 1993, Thames Television. Now only vestiges remain of the former road network: eg **DIANA PLACE**, first shown on Horwood's map of 1793, is now a service road through the centre of the complex. The sole building remaining within Triton Square is at **No.40**, being the Wembley College of Central London, a post-WW II block. **SEATON PLACE** is now but a pedestrian walkway skirting the north face of Euston Tower and marking the site of Seaton Street, renamed in 1886 after local Vestryman John Lewis Seaton, at that time proprietor of a furniture warehouse at 93-95 Hampstead Road. In Charles Booth's 1889 *Survey of London Poverty* Seaton Street was classified as an area inhabited by the lowest class – vicious and semicriminal – the only place so rated in the area covered by this book. By contrast, the houses fronting the Euston Road and Hampstead Road were classified as well-to-do, middle class, with only the occasional mention of very poor inhabitants (cf p 39).

The University of Westminster (formerly Polytechnic of Central London) School of Languages now stands with the **Goat and Boots** public house on the corner of Triton Square, where al fresco drinkers can enjoy a view of the entrance to the huge Euston Centre underground car park, the entrance being close to the site of the former Goat in Boots at 31 Stanhope Street. Earlier industrial and commercial properties on the north side of Drummond Street, such as the Eagle Brewery and several large works, have vanished. At No.178-182, now a derelict site used to park cars, was the site of Lush's Flats and Regent's Park Free Church put up by Lady Lush, a devoted and wealthy Baptist, to provide a meeting centre and home for the poor women of the neighbourhood. On one corner of Stanhope Street is **Kingsway College**, built in 1976 as the Stanhope Institute. On this site early in the 20th century was the Regent's Park Central Electric Power Station. With this DC system, St Pancras was the first Municipal Authority to supply electricity to private consumers. Tottenham Court Road was first lit with twelve arc lamps (mounted in the centre of the road) in January 1892. In the **LONGFORD STREET** garden of Kingsway College is a 1976 statue, *Seated Boy*, by Jean Bullock. Southwest beyond the statue, the marked change in building style marks the boundary of the Crown Estate, which crosses Longford Street at an oblique angle and disappears north behind the College and through the housing estate.

First on the right in **STANHOPE STREET** is the **Lord Nelson** pub which, a plaque records, was established in 1803 and rebuilt in 1899. On the same block there survive four original terraced houses (**Nos.50-52, 58-60**). Opposite the Lord Nelson is the **Samuel Lithgow Boys' Club**, named after the founder of the Stanhope Institute for Working Men and Women, founded in 1891 at No.86 Stanhope Street between William and Netley Streets and later in Triton Square. The Boys' Club building backs onto the Regent's Park Estate, dominated here by the 70 flats in 20 storeys of **Bucklebury**.

Former Stanhope Street residents included the actor Charles Macready, who was born in 1793 at No.45, but his plaque disappeared when the house was

Streets Renamed

Present name	Former name
Present name	*Former name*
Drummond St [W]	Charles Street
Euston Road	The New Road
Granby Terrace	Granby Street
Mackworth Street	Rutland Street
North Gower Street	George Street
Seaton Place	Seaton Street
	earlier Henry Street
Stanhope Street [S]	Brook Street
[middle]	Mary Street
Varndell Street	Edward Street
William Road	William Street

demolished in 1965. The sculptors Mary Thornycroft and her husband Thomas lived at No.39 in the 1850s. Thomas's best-known statue is probably Boadicea in her chariot beside Westminster Bridge; Mary was known for her many statues and busts of the Royal Family. No.53 Stanhope

Street was the home of Matthew Flinders, who explored Australian and Tasmanian coasts around 1800. He is commemorated by the Flinders River and the Flinders Range; his plaque was removed at the 1965 demolition to another of his Camden residences, 56 Fitzroy Street at the junction with Warren Street.

HAMPSTEAD ROAD, to which we now return, continues to be the main highway north through Camden Town. Bus services ran from Euston Road to Camden Town as early as the 1840s. A horse-drawn tramway was built along the route (and on to Kentish Town) in 1871/72, when the single fare was 1d outside and 2d inside. Electric trams were introduced in 1909, but the Euston Road marked the northern limit of 'Central London' from which trams were banned, so the tramlines terminated at the southern end of Hampstead Road. At **No.66** survives a gem of a 5-storey house, the sole survivor of Victorian terraces on this side of the road. On the southeast corner with Drummond Street is the shell of the Lord Palmerston public house, now occupied by the Unity Theatre and Camden Council offices; this is all that remains of the frontage that once extended to the (old) Euston Road as the former Tolmers Square, with its Chapel (later a cinema) in the centre and surrounding terraces which were demolished in the 1970s despite a massive local protest campaign. Tolmers

Square was itself built on the site of the reservoir formed by the New River Company in 1797. The main building on the site is now the mirror-glass-finished **Prudential Building.**

Former residents of this area included Captain John Mills of the East India Company, whose gravestone in St Pancras churchyard records that he was the last survivor of the Black Hole of Calcutta (1756) and lived, said the *Gentleman's Magazine,* in Hampstead Road from 1802 until his death in 1811. In 1797 a distinguished lodger at 12 Hampstead Road (on the east side near the New Road) was Vicomte François René de Chateaubriand, fugitive from the French Revolutionary Terror in 1794. He returned to France in 1800 and reappeared in London in 1821 as the French Ambassador, this time living luxuriously in Portland Place. On the northwest junction with Drummond Street is the rebuilt **Sol's Arms** which replaced an earlier pub of that name which, Walford's *Old and New London* tells us, is derived from the Sol's Society, a long disbanded group of the Freemason type. Dickens used the name for the public house where the inquest was held in the second chapter of *Bleak House,* but located it in Lincoln's Inn. Our old pub was at No.1 Sol's Row and at No.10, later 83, Hampstead Road. Most of Sol's Row (and some of the Drummond Street frontage)

was taken over by Oetzmann's furniture store (1860s until the mid-1950s). Within the block 89-105 Hampstead Road (once Frederick Place) only **103** and **105** remain of the original houses, again with shops built onto the fronts at street level. The furniture tradition of the locality remains, with office furniture showrooms (and the Sol's Arms) taking the ground floor frontage of the 1950s block (refurbished 1980s), whose upper storeys are occupied by the Logica software company.

Moving north we pass **WILLIAM ROAD** (after William IV) which once had residential frontages but is now totally commercial on the north side. The large Volvo Agency was until 1945 the Maples Garage, like so many other properties of the time supporting the local furniture and piano trade. By 1880 Maples at the top end of Tottenham Court Road was the largest furniture house in Britain. In WW II **Nos.20-22** William Road were the wartime 'Ambulance Station 50' known in St Pancras Civil Defence circles as 'the Indian Station' because the Station Officer spoke several Indian languages. On the north side, the 5-storey block of 20 Victorian flats named **Hampstead House** (1892) is the sole original building. The rest of the frontage includes the 1974 extension to Netley Street Primary School, submerged at basement level of the houses destroyed by bombing.

The primary school's main entrance is

at the end of the next turning, **NETLEY STREET**, now a cul-de-sac with new houses and redeveloped **PRINCE REGENT MEWS** on the south side and Victorian buildings opposite. Two small original houses survive as **Nos.37,38** just short of the grand original **Netley Street School** built for the London School Board in 1883. The original separate entrances for Boys, Girls and Infants survive. In 1889 Booth's classification of the area between Netley and Robert Streets was very poor, casual – chronic want, this being only one grade above the lowest class (cf p 37).

Back in Hampstead Road the Victorian houses at **Nos.111-117** had shops built on their fronts but Nos.111-115 were an empty site in 1994. On the upper brickwork of No.117 can be seen the name J Bryce Smith, a popular shop for artists' materials in the 1930s. The narrow **PRINCE OF WALES PASSAGE** (named for the one who became George IV) leads under the side of the **Prince of Wales** public house to the cobbled **EVERTON BUILDINGS** (formerly William Mews), its early 20th-century buildings on the south side now used for special educational purposes by the Education Authority. The new (1990s) building of oriental appearance on the corner of Robert Street is the home of the Bengali Workers Association, providing social, welfare and educational service for the local Bengali community.

It is worth crossing to the east side of Hampstead Road to inspect the buildings and park. At **No.108** is the former St Pancras Female Orphanage, established in 1776 and rebuilt on this site in 1904. This, like the whole of the former Temperance Hospital to the north, is used for offices and certain 'outreach' services of the Camden and Islington Health Authority Trust, but **Jimmy's Café** on the ground floor is open to the public. The quiet **St James's Gardens** to the rear were established by a 1788 Act of Parliament as an additional burial ground for St James's, Piccadilly, and the space was opened as public gardens in 1887 by the St Pancras Vestry. Here lie the painters George Morland and John Hoppner, Lord George Gordon of Gordon Riots notoriety (see *Camden History Review 8*), and Matthew Flinders (p 38).

St James's Chapel, by Thomas Hardwick, consecrated in 1791, was the parish church where George Gissing married Nellie Harrison in 1879. It stood until 1956, the cleared site now being the central courtyard of the former Temperance Hospital, which ceased to function as a hospital in the early 1980s. Founded in 1873 with only 17 beds in a private house at 112 Gower Street, this moved in 1881 to a corner site just north of St James's Chapel, replacing the St Pancras Female Charity School, built in 1790 on ground given by Lord

Southampton. In 1904 a Nurses' Home was built on the site in exuberant Edwardian style. The Insull Wing to the south was donated by Samuel Insull, who emigrated to America and became Edison's assistant. As the foundation stone of the Temperance Hospital (dated May 1879) states, it was built '... for the treatment of medical and surgical case without the use of alcohol'. In fact, by 1948 252 of the 83,000 in-patients treated *had* been given alcohol as part of their treatment.

Cardington Street is the approximate site of the turnpike shown in Rowlandson's 1798 cartoon (p 66). To the north, on the opposite side of Hampstead Road, we see all post-WW II buildings, such as **Silverdale**, an 8-storey block of flats on a site where Alfred Tennyson is said to have lodged on a visit to London in 1850. He left behind the manuscript of *In Memoriam* which, by a stroke of luck, Coventry Patmore was able to recover for him.

Recross Hampstead Road and traverse **ROBERT STREET**, which is now the only thoroughfare between Hampstead Road and Albany Street. The sculptor Alfred Stevens, designer of the Wellington monument in St Paul's, first lived and worked at No.10 Robert Street in 1844, while one of Walter Sickert's many Camden studios was at No.13 in 1898. In 1934 there were artists at Nos.9,11 and 13 while the Hampstead artist C R W Nevinson had a studio in Robert Street in 1917-18. All these studios have now gone and have been replaced by the terraces and tower blocks with picturesque Lakeland names (see p 32).

STANHOPE STREET north of Robert Street is entirely post-1945 housing with a few shops at Stanhope Parade and **The Sovereign** (Elizabeth I) pub, while the **Regent's Park Nursery Centre** operates above the concrete garage now used for the secure storage of new cars. As an infant the actress Ellen Terry lived with her family at No.92 (pre-1868 numbering) in the 1850s, at the north end of the street, near Granby Terrace. At the junction is 100 Park Village East, the headquarters since 1985 of the Policy Studies Institute. One of Walter Sickert's many studios overlooked this area and in an article in *The New Age* in 1914 he recalled that he had once seen a man 'standing with a cheroot in one hand, looking out towards the light with his head slightly raised, half in pleasure ... he had got to be drawn ... before the sun sets behind the houses of Stanhope Street and puts a cold extinguisher of lead on the whole scene...'. One consolation for the light cut off nowadays in Stanhope Street by the high-rise buildings is that it could have been a lot worse if Professor Abercrombie's 1943 County of London Plan had been implemented: this proposed feeding the main north-south route for cross-London traffic down from Swiss Cottage and along an arterial road where Stanhope Street now is, to enter a tunnel around Robert Street which would run under Gower Street and surface in Covent Garden. Worse, in 1970 a feeder road to the projected Inner Motorway Box was planned to run along the lines of Mornington Terrace and Oval Road to join the Box over Camden Lock.

VARNDELL STREET was Edward Street until 1938. No.21 Edward Street and 15-16 Robert Mews backing on to it (now occupied by the garden at the rear of **Staveley**) were leased in 1832 by Lord Southampton to the Southampton Paving Trust Commissioners (to repair the roads on his estate) as a board room and offices. St Pancras Vestry succeeded them and let the premises in 1860 to the 3rd Volunteer Battalion, Royal Fusiliers on a lease which expired in 1921, when the Vestry had become the St Pancras Borough Council. These buildings are all gone. The **King's Head**, on the north side, is successor to two earlier inns, the George IV, which was licensed as a theatre in 1854-60, and the Crown and Sceptre, rather later, on the opposite side of the road.

HARRINGTON STREET, dating from about 1830, was named after the Earl of Harrington who gave his family name to Stanhope Street. The street is now lined with post-WW II flats and has a pedestrian archway through to Granby Terrace. In the northern part of Harrington Street an interesting character called Timothy Claxton died in 1848. He came from Bungay in Suffolk and started a Mechanics' Institute about 1817, an early date for such a body. He went to Russia and helped build the St Petersburg gas works, then to America where he played a part in American Mechanics' Institutes and wrote a short autobiography called *Memoirs of a Mechanic*. An obituary in 1849 described him as a 'useful working man', whose house was fitted up with all manner of lathes, rotary saws and similar equipment.

MACKWORTH STREET, a companion to Granby Street, once ran through to the Hampstead Road and was named Rutland Street when built in about 1830 until 1938, when it was named after Sir Thomas Mackworth, buried in St Pancras churchyard in 1744.

GRANBY TERRACE was Granby Street until 1937 and took its name from the Granby Arms. This pub, together with houses on both sides of the road, was swept away from 1889 onwards by successive widenings of the railway, which crosses obliquely under the road. The broadening of the cutting to accommodate the carriage sheds in 1900 meant that bridges extending across the railway to Park Village East from the southern end of Mornington Terrace and from Mornington

Place had to be removed; instead, a connection was made across the Crown Estate boundary from the southern end of Park Village East to the junction of Stanhope Street and Granby Terrace, and a new bridge was built as an extension of Mornington Street. The present red and blue brick railway buildings serve the extensive carriage sheds below. There are 12 'roads' (ie tracks), each a third of a mile in length, so the sheds could hold over 120 railway carriages. Now operated by Rail Express Systems, the depot maintains the overnight mail carriages. At one time the depot was known as the Old Port Arthur Depot as many of its workers joined the Merchant Navy in 1914 and they returned with a huge bell which was proudly displayed until stolen – but the bell support remains aloft in the carriage works.

The small three-storey Victorian **Granby House** behind an iron gate and down a short path (once Granby Yard) between high walls off the stub of Mackworth Street is of railway origin, probably the former office of railway officials with accommodation above. Granby Terrace (then Street) itself once housed the Scottish journalist and novelist William Black who, in 1870, was arrested as a spy in Germany where he was reporting the Franco-Prussian War for the Morning Star. Before leaving Granby Terrace, look south to handsome Stalbridge House overlooking the tracks at 213 Hampstead Road. It is a

brick building of 20 (originally railway company) flats in five storeys built in 1909. The flats in the upper storey and the roof were destroyed by a fire in 1976, but without loss of life.

The **Euston Taxi Centre** on the Hampstead Road junction is a long-established parking lot for a small number of London cabs and is on a derelict site behind advertisement hoardings where once there were seven terraced houses. The first of these was the Wellington House Academy where Charles Dickens was at school from 1825 to 1827. Twenty years later he wrote that the railway took 'the playground, sliced the schoolroom and pared off the corner of the house'. Later on Walter Sickert painted and taught in the house, No.247 Hampstead Road, which bore a plaque to Dickens in 1924 but had to be demolished in 1964 for bridge rebuilding. **Nos.261** and **263** are the only remaining houses of an elegant terrace of about 1830, which gave a fitting introduction to Mornington Crescent. **No.263** bears a plaque to the artist George Cruikshank, who lived here from 1850 until his death in 1878 (but see Augustus Street, p 27). Another celebrated artist, Clarkson Stanfield, previously in Mornington Crescent (p 61), lived in the same house in 1846 before moving to Hampstead. The house was then 48 Mornington Place.

Across the Hampstead Road from the

end of Granby Terrace are three 20-storey tower blocks. The railway here covers most of what was once respectable Victorian Ampthill Square, the Hampstead Road entrance to which was at the centre of the office/warehouse buildings at **No.132-140**. The original 140 Hampstead Road was a substantial end-of-terrace house, rented 1910-14 by Walter Sickert and named by him 'Rowlandson House' after the great comic draughtsman who illustrated the road (p 66). No.138 is the site of the farmhouse of the notorious St Pancras Vestryman Thomas Rhodes (see *Camden History Review 2*), who farmed many acres of land on both the Crown and Southampton estates. His brother was Cecil Rhodes, who gave his name to Rhodesia (now Zimbabwe) and raised a tomb to the family in St Pancras Churchyard. The farmhouse survived until about 1943.

The striking building on the west side of Hampstead Road was built as their 'Arcadia Works' by the Carreras Cigarette Company on what had been the gardens of Mornington Crescent. Constructed in 1926 in a style inspired by the discovery of Tutankhamun's tomb, the 550-ft long building was known as the 'Black Cat Factory' after the two giant bronze cats which originally guarded the main entrance and the brand of cigarettes produced. The factory is a stylized copy of the temple of Bubastis, the cat-headed goddess of ancient Egypt. The building, later the 'Craven A' works (see advertisement below) was designed by M E and O H Collins and is described by Pevsner as 'abominable'. It employed over 3000 workers on 9 acres of floor space. It was later used by the Greater London Council until its abolition in the 1980s, and is now used as offices by a number of businesses, mostly in the advertising field.

Opposite, on the east side of **HARRINGTON SQUARE**, where now stands **Hurdwick House**, was the terrace where George Medals were won by members of the St Pancras ARP Service after a German bomb fell in the early hours of 9 September 1940. It demolished three houses, blew a crater in the road, and up-ended a double-decker bus. The passengers had just taken cover in the trenches dug in the square at the time of the Munich Crisis in 1938. These were also damaged by the blast, and 11 people were killed. In another wartime incident in the square a German parachute mine became suspended from the chimney pots, but

luckily failed to explode. Possibly the worst night of the blitz was that of 10/11 May 1941 when bombs demolished many of the houses in nearby streets and damaged the Hampstead Road railway bridge.

To the north of Harrington Square is **Mornington Crescent station**, with its glazed red tiles, opened in 1907 on the site of Millbrook Place.

And so we come to the corner of Mornington Crescent, at the southernmost point of the walk described in Section 3B.

This advertisement seeking labour for the Arcadia Works emphasised health benefits for staff in this cigarette factory which blighted Mornington Crescent

THE WORLD FAMOUS HOME OF THE WORLD'S MOST FAMOUS CORK-TIPPED CIGARETTES — *Craven 'A'*

Working under ideal conditions each employee has the advantage of every modern facility for the betterment of health, education and recreation including :— Full-time Medical Officer, Dentist and trained nurses, expert treatment by oculist and chiropodist. Holiday home at Brighton, Day School classes for all under 18. Financial assistance for adults continuing their studies. Free legal advice. An H.S.A. Group and Works Library. Four canteens and tea (without charge) at morning and afternoon rest breaks. Large Sports Ground at Stanmore with Bowls, Cricket, Tennis, Football and Netball Clubs; also club sections for Angling, Bridge, Darts, Horticulture, Amateur Dramatics and Swimming.

Section 3 East of the Railway

(see map 1 at end of book)

The effect of two major early 19th-century transport developments on the area

THE AREA between the Round House at Chalk Farm and the Hampstead Road Bridge, known to be rural fields and estates in the early 1800s, became the site of large-scale industrial development and associated low-cost housing during the first part of the 19th century. First came the construction of the Regent's Canal as far as Camden Town, between the years 1814 and 1816, en route to the Thames at Limehouse. It was followed by the arrival of the London and Birmingham Railway in the 1830s, with the subsequent extensive growth of the Camden Goods Yard.

Chalk Farm Bridge over the two-track London and Birmingham Railway, 1840. At this point the locomotive is able to haul the train; from Euston this required the Stationary Engines whose chimneys are shown on the right.

Businesses were established in the surrounding area to service the new transport lines and distribute the goods arriving by rail and water, so that a complex of warehouses, stables and sheds was created.

The Regent's Canal

Paddington Basin, the London end of the Grand Junction Canal, had by the early 1800s been established as a major depot for manufactured and agricultural goods to and from the Midlands. The Canal was extended as the Regent's Canal all the way to the Regent's Canal Dock at Limehouse, where the goods could be transferred directly to ships. There were early problems for the Canal Company. At Camden Lock an experimental hydro-pneumatic lock, designed to save water on passage of a vessel, had to be abandoned in 1812. The three traditional locks, which are still operable, were completed in 1819. Other problems included litigation and wrangling over compensation with William Agar, a local landowner, and a major embezzlement by Thomas Homer, one of the originators of the canal. These difficulties, compounded by the competition of the railway, resulted in the Canal Company never being as profitable as expected, though goods were still being carried, in diminished tonnage, until 1960. It is now given over to leisure activities.

The area around the canal basins forms the focus of the Camden Lock Market, where a multiplicity of stalls attract huge crowds every weekend. This market has largely taken over from the King's Road, Chelsea as a mecca for young people. The imposing buildings in the area no longer used by the railways include the Roundhouse and the Interchange Warehouse.

The Railways

At the peak of its importance the Camden Goods Yard area, concealed behind the high wall along Chalk Farm Road, was scored by a myriad of rail tracks. Authorised by Parliament in 1833, the original double track of the London and Birmingham Railway was to terminate at Camden Town. Like the Canal Company, the Railways encountered early difficulties with land purchase. Four years later the need to link with central London led Parliament to empower the London and Birmingham Railway to construct an extension from Camden Goods Yard, south of Gloucester Avenue, to Euston Grove. However, as the Regent's Canal could not be breached by a railway cutting but had to be crossed by a bridge only 800 yards from the terminus at the much lower level of Euston Road, the incline to Euston was too great for the then power of the locomotives. The railway engineer Robert Stephenson's solution to these problems was to build the Stationary Engine House beneath the rail track, alongside the Goods Yard. It was a cavern 163 ft wide, topped by two 130-ft chimneys which extracted the furnace smoke from the huge steam-powered engines. The carriages were detached and rolled down the incline with men acting as brakemen. On the upward return, men pushed the carriages as far as the bridge just outside Euston, and then engaged the mile-long rope to winch the carriages to the Goods Yard. This rope was 7 inches in diameter and some 12 tons in weight. The whole procedure became a tourist attraction.

This spectacular feat of engineering became obsolete by 1844 because Stephenson developed engines which could cope with the incline. Euston was established as the passenger terminal; Chalk Farm stored and fuelled the locomotives. The winding engines were sold to a flax mill in Russia. The division of our area by railways continued in 1851, when a new railway, initially called The East and West India Docks and Birmingham Junction Railway, was built as a freight connection for Birmingham traffic to the London Docks. From Camden Town Station (now Camden Road Station) it crossed to Hampstead Road Station (later Chalk Farm Station and then Primrose Hill Station). When it proved successful also as a passenger line for workers commuting to the City the name was changed (1853) to the North London Railway. Primrose Hill Station was closed to passengers in 1992 and the line that passes under Chalk Farm Road close to the Canal is now used solely for freight.

These major lines of transport were the cause of massive growth of both domestic and commercial building. Land that was once fields was sold off for development. One of the largest landowners, Lord Southampton, sold off part of his estates here at a historic sale in 1840 for an average price of £300 per acre. The housing needed for the railway workers (many of whom were the progenitors of today's 'Camden Irish' population) and subsequently for those using the railway station, later named Primrose Hill, resulted in a rash of new houses.

A major commercial concern in the area, which appears often in our survey, was Gilbey's, the Wine Importer and Spirit Distiller. From a small wine import company set up in Scotland in 1857 by brothers Walter and Alfred, Gilbey's grew to cover 20 acres in Camden by 1914. In 1876, 7 years after arriving in Camden they had two bonded warehouses - a building in the stables yard (demolished 1960) and the Round House - and an export warehouse, bottle warehouse and distillery across the Canal on Oval and Jamestown Roads.

Chalk Farm Tube Station to Parkway

(see map 1 at end of book)

THIS WALK starts at the northeast corner of our survey. At Chalk Farm Underground station we are at one of the oldest road junctions in the whole area: where the ancient northbound road begins the climb to Hampstead, a footpath to the original Chalk Farm Tavern joined it from the southwest. Now the footpath is again for pedestrians only, who have to climb over the railway bridge, closed to cars, to reach the present-day successor of the Tavern (p 72). As we look south, Adelaide Road leads off to the right towards Swiss Cottage, and immediately across the road rises the bulk of the Round House behind a high brick wall.

The **Round House** on **CHALK FARM ROAD** (renamed from 'Pancras Vale' in 1865) is an outstanding example of Camden's railway history. In 1840 Robert Dockray, a Quaker born in 1811 in Cumberland, became the resident engineer of the London and Birmingham Railway (eventually to become part of the London, Midland and Scottish Railway), under Robert Stephenson. He was living in a house in Pancras Vale in 1846 when he designed the Round House as a repair shed for engines. Through an entrance on the west side an engine would be moved to the central turntable and from there transferred to one of 23 bays for inspection and service. The diameter of the building is 160 ft and its lantern-topped roof was, and is, supported by 24 equally spaced cast iron columns. The total floor area is 20,000 sq ft.

As engines became too long to fit into the bays, the Round House became obsolete and was used as a goods shed by firms like Pickfords and later Gilbey's, the Wine and Spirit Merchants (p 46). Gilbey's ceased occupation in 1963. Later that year a 16-year lease was donated to Arnold Wesker, playwright and idealist, who founded a community arts project called Centre 42. The Round House Trustees, set up in 1965, were able to buy the freehold for £27,500. After Wesker left in 1970 the arts theme continued with plays and concerts. The Theatre Downstairs was opened in 1975 and the main theatre auditorium was updated in 1979. However, despite Arts and Camden Council grants, it had to close when subsidies ceased in 1983. Camden Council and the GLC bought the freehold back for £330,000. Plans were put in hand to turn the Round House into a Black Arts Centre, but although large sums of money were channelled into the project, this had to be abandoned in 1990. In 1992 Camden Council sold the Round House to a property developer for £895,000 to renovate and reinstate it as a leading arts venue. In 1994 English Heritage again expressed concern about the building's continued deterioration and describe it as 'vulnerable'. Plans to re-open the Round House as an auditorium to seat 2,500 people are yet to be realised. At the time of writing, the Round House is open only occasionally at weekends for stalls, though the opportunity to climb the short stone flight of steps to the main entrance should not be missed.

Adjacent to the Round House, Richard Seifert's glass-fronted office block was built in the mid-1970s. On the opposite side of the street stretches a parade of shops sited on what would originally have been the small front gardens of the modest yellow-brick terraced houses built there in the late 1830s. Included in the range of small businesses is a piano showroom, a

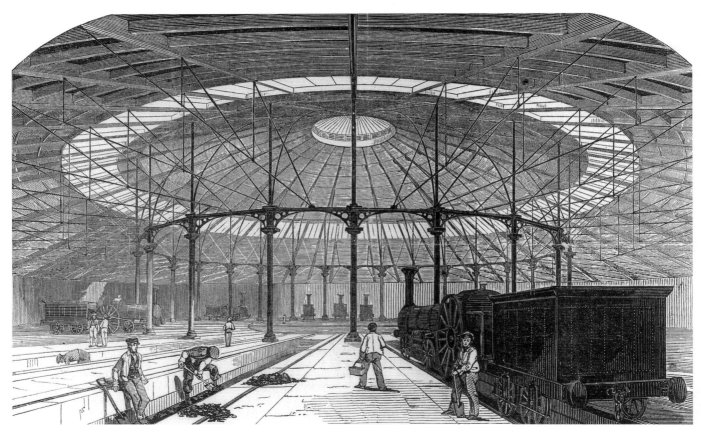

48

reminder of Camden's former importance as a centre of piano manufacturing. According to the 1889-90 Street Directory there was a pianoforte makers at **No.77**, which later became the Belmont Inn, renamed in 1991 as **The Engine Room**. Other public houses on the east side of the road include the **Monarch** on the corner of Ferdinand Street, with its sign of Queen Victoria, and **The Man in the Moon**, first opened in 1991. The **Lock Tavern** on the corner with Harmood Street was originally called the Railway Tavern. Its re-naming in 1982 shows how much things had changed. A 1905 photograph of the building shows an elaborate wrought-iron railing on the upper floor terrace and the front gardens of the houses to the right. Opposite the pub is Thomson's the pawnbrokers, established in 1837 and still displaying the three golden balls. Past the petrol station the two rows of shops on either side of Hawley Street, **Nos.10-18** and **20-26**, are shown as Hampton Terrace on Daw's 1849 parish map of St Pancras. Furniture shops, boutiques and cafes now abound to serve the thousands of people visiting the Camden Lock market each week.

Old railway land on the west side is due to support a supermarket in 1995, the main access to which will be through an

Interior of the Round House
(Illustrated London News, 1856)

opening in a long high wall, which originally ran the length of Chalk Farm Road and for 100 years concealed the railway tracks and warehouses from the public.

Further south along the wall lies the cobbled entrance to former stables and warehouses. The dilapidated buildings reveal many of their original features, such as a horse ramp for second-storey access and iron hoists for the transfer of goods. The four blocks were built in 1855 to replace an original complex of stables destroyed by an 1853 fire. The rail and canal companies, and later on other firms, shared the stabling and warehouses under the arches. It is interesting to note that in 1869 Gilbey's leased a shed for £2100 a year and that in 1881 as many as 420 horses were kept in the stable complex. The necessary manure pit was against the high Chalk Farm Road wall, and its smell must have carried into the street beyond. The **horse hospital**, with cobbled floor and stalls with sliding doors, can still be seen at the top of the slope to the north, beside an Underground carriage which has lost its way.

Beneath the railway tracks is a network of brick-lined barrel-vaulted tunnels, for the passage of horses from the stables to their work. Nowadays market traders at the weekend place their stalls against the outer walls of the buildings; several of the blocks are too dangerous to enter. Public access

is denied during the week.

Continuing to follow the wall along Chalk Farm Road under the railway bridge, and noting the row of semicircular windows of the warehouse behind, we enter **CAMDEN LOCK PLACE**, formerly Commercial Place, where the wharves and warehouses were built to service the Canal. Many of the buildings of the U-shaped West Yard around the small canal basin are, apart from the cosmetic additions of balconies and ironwork walkways, much the same as when they were built. The central stable block was leased in 1937 to T E Dingwall Ltd, who manufactured packing cases and took delivery of timber from the canal. Since the 1970s the area has developed as a market, with craft shops and stalls. The Dingwalls building (p 51) is a popular music venue. It was renovated in 1991, with a new pub on the upper floor and room for 500 people in the auditorium below. Such refurbishment was stimulated by the 1980s development boom and the increasing popularity of the market with tourists and young people. The **New Market Hall** was opened in 1991. Designed in keeping with its surroundings by John Dickinson, with an interior inspired by the Gas Hall in Birmingham, it was built on a concrete frame, clad with reclaimed bricks. A bridge joins it to the new building in the West Yard.

Canal pleasure boat trips further

encourage visitors to the site. The **TOWPATH** forms an interesting walk eastwards to York Way and westwards to Lisson Grove. There is access to the towpath beside the Canal basin in the West Yard via a gate; beside the New Market Hall via steps; and from the south side of the canal bridge, beside the lock-keeper's neo-Gothic house and over the decorative iron bridge (*opposite*).

Follow the towpath west, noticing how the path arches above the level of the water to allow barge access to the basin beneath the prominent Interchange Building on the right. Across the canal is a disused wharf where rubbish from the GLC refuse transfer station (now the Recycling Centre, p 55) on Jamestown Road used to be loaded onto canal barges. The white building with iron stairs and balconies, of faintly transatlantic liner aspect, is the rear of Gilbey's warehouse and bottling plant (see Jamestown Road). The steps on the far side of Southampton Bridge lead to Oval Road.

The perfectly straight **OVAL ROAD** gets its name from the oval which would have been formed by two crescents on either side, only one of which (Gloucester Crescent, on the east) was built. The coming of the railway in the 1830s prevented the construction of a similar crescent on the west.

At the north end of Oval Road a stretch of waste ground leading into the old Camden Goods Yard is scheduled for the supermarket and new housing; it will have access from Chalk Farm Road. Remains of weighbridges mark the entrance to railway land. Traces can be seen of rail tracks and the circular iron gratings which lit the tunnels from the stables and warehouses on Chalk Farm Road. The first Victorian three-storey warehouse, **No.30**, now houses Henson's (of Muppets and Spitting Image fame) Creatures Shop. Its dingy brickwork contrasts with the recently sandblasted multicoloured brickwork of the **Interchange Building**.

This is a grade II, five-storey late Victorian warehouse dating between 1891 and 1913. The Interchange was first used to move goods between rail and canal, and subsequently for storage. A rectangular basin directly under the building feeds from the canal; doors and bays on either side, and the square cast-iron supports which run down the middle of the basin, have been retained by the designers who renovated the building in 1989-90. It is occupied partly by World Television News.

On the west side of Oval Road, beside the canal, is **The Pirate Castle**. This was built in 1977, to an uncharacteristic design of Sir Richard Seifert in mock fortress style, to house the Pirate Club, founded by Lord St Davids. The club was used to instruct boys and girls in canoeing and rowing, but was closed early in 1994 because of concentration of Council funding on the Jubilee Club to the east along the canal. The Electricity Board has built a pumping station in a harmonious style on the opposite side of the canal.

The building on the corner with Jamestown Road, **Nos.24-28**, previously occupied by the Stanhope Arms public house, was designed as Gilbey's offices by Mendelsohn and Chermayeff in 1937. Innovative features such as soundproofing and air conditioning were incorporated. The numerous small windows were designed to give plenty of natural light without compromising the available interior space.

On the west side of Oval Road, south of the canal, was a Potato Market (Goad's Insurance map of 1870). The land was taken over in the later 1870s by Gilbey's as part of their distilling empire, for vatting and blending wines and spirits. In a later edition of the map two subways are shown running between the Gilbey sites on opposite sides of the road. It is now an office block (**No.35**) with rear warehouse.

Three yellow-brick terrace houses opposite, **Nos.14-18 Oval Road**, have interesting wrought-iron balconies. Note the iron coalhole covers in the pavement in

Camden (triple) Lock today, looking west. Centre left, Gilbey's warehouse and bottling plant. On the right, the refurbished Interchange Building and Dingwall's former factory, now a pub and music venue.

front of the entrances. **No.12** is a renovated office block, built during the 1880s but refurbished in the 'Art Deco' style. Next to it on the corner with Gloucester Crescent is an imposing 22-sided building by Thomas and William Piper, dating from the mid-19th century, formerly known as The Old Piano Factory but now as **The Rotunda**. The original building, similar in shape but lower, was burned down in 1851 within a year of construction. It was built to house Collard and Collard, one of Camden's leading piano manufacturers, and originally had a central hoist for completed pianos. It was renovated in 1991, unfortunately with an out-of-keeping porch over the main entrance. Now Grade II-listed, it has housed two publishers, Duckworths and Virago.

No.31 on the west side dates from 1936; it was used as a canteen for railway workers and the carriers Pickfords, who had a large depot in Camden Goods Yard. The new frontage was added in 1986. The Camden Society of Architects has its address here.

The handsome terrace of houses **Nos. 2-10** on the east side retains many original features, including iron balconies at either end of the block. Next to them and set back from the road is elegant **REGENT'S PARK TERRACE**, built in the 1840s by Oldfield (see also p 77) with delightful ironwork balconies. Samuel Cousins, the mezzotint engraver, lived at **No.12** in the 1850s: he was the first man to receive the rank of academician engraver. Louis Kossuth, the Hungarian patriot, stayed in this same house in 1861.

The row of four substantial semi-detached houses, **Nos.3-17**, opposite Regent's Park Terrace were built between 1860 and 1868. They reflect an earlier 19th century design of town house, with Doric-columned porches to one side. At the end of Oval Road, on the west side, is a group of houses, **Nos.1A-E**, with garages on the ground floor and roof gardens above, which were designed by Ted Levy, Benjamin & Partners in the 1960s to fit onto a very narrow tapering site between the road and the railway.

PARKWAY was known as Slipshoe Lane in the 18th century; when there were no houses it was no doubt muddy. In the 19th century it became Park Street, and an early row of houses at the west end was called Stanhope Terrace. The truncated remains of these (between the junctions with Delancey Street and Park Village East) still exist as **Nos.119-125 Parkway**. Half of Stanhope Terrace had to go for railway widening, and the name was abolished after 1937, when the whole street was named Parkway. The street is now notable for estate agents, boutiques and cafés. It is well supplied with pubs, of which the **Dublin Castle** at No. 94 is a pleasant early stucco-faced building and the **Spread Eagle** at Nos. 57-59 is also mid-19th century. The 'Camden Stores' public house on the corner of Arlington Road, refurbished and reopened as the **Rat and Parrot** in 1994, has an inscription for the brewery Truman, Hanbury and Buxton & Co dated 1924.

Through the archway by **No.77** was a group of buildings associated with piano making and sheet-music printers (Lowe & Brydon). Conversion of some of the Victorian warehouses in the courtyard into offices in 1975 won an award; the remaining warehouse was renovated as offices in 1985-86.

No.73 was a watchmaker's, a tobacconist and from 1863 a confectioner for 60 years. Note the curious architraves round the upper windows. It is now the **Regent Bookshop** where Camden History Society publications are stocked. The famous firm of Robertson & Co who made artists' paints were based at **No.71** from 1936 until the mid-1980s. The company, established in 1810 in Long Acre, made colours for the pre-Raphaelites and many notable painters of the 19th century, supplying them to no fewer than six Presidents of the Royal Academy. The building is now an estate agent's. **No.35** is **Palmer's Regent's Pet Store**, founded in 1918 by George Palmer. In 1969 a photograph of the manager with a boa constrictor appeared in a local paper which reported that the snake and her 20 babies were set loose in the shop at night to deter intruders!

Further down the street on the opposite side, past the junction with Arlington Road, is the site of the Alexandra Theatre. Opened in 1873 and later called the Park Theatre, it was destroyed by fire in 1881. The Royal Park Hall was erected on the site and used as a meeting place/entertainment hall, but was later converted into a workshop and cabinet factory. In 1936-37 a Gaumont Cinema was built in its place, later becoming the Odeon. In 1984 the cinema was reopened as the Parkway Centre and in 1985 a second smaller screen was added called the Regency. In 1987, when the lease ran out, the cinema was closed in anticipation of the redevelopment of the surrounding area by Landmark Properties despite protest by local residents. When the proposed development fell through the cinema was reopened in 1989. The reprieve was short-lived and again, despite protest, the cinema was closed in August 1993.

No.5 with its distinctive columns and doorways was for 44 years from 1874 the London and South Western Bank, subsequently Barclays Bank. In 1990 the building was converted to a new music venue, the Jazz Café, which creates a luxurious atmosphere by clever use of lighting on painted steel, concrete and linoleum surfaces. Opposite at **No.10** is the Post Office and between **No.6-8** is an alleyway with a fine ironwork gate which

originally led to a tram depot. **No.6** is reputed to be the first premises of the ABC bakery, which moved to larger premises on what is now the Camden Sainsbury's site.

At the junction of Parkway with the High Street are the **Ladies' Toilets** which first appeared here in 1883, after campaigning by the Ladies' Sanitary Association and support from George Bernard Shaw.

Now we backtrack up Parkway and turn right into the northernmost stretch of **ARLINGTON ROAD**. Originally named Grove Street, along with its southern continuation on the other side of Parkway, there were houses on both sides of the street by the 1820s. On the west side **No.173** houses the Camden Chinese Community Centre. The Cavendish School is approached through an arch beside **No.179**. This was originally St Mark's School, associated with St Mark's Church (p 84), and the emblem of St Mark (a winged lion) graces the front of the building, which was refurbished in 1992. First opened in 1855, it was transferred to St Michael's Church, Camden Town, in 1901 on adjustment of parish boundaries, and the premises were bought from the Church of England by the Roman Catholic Church in 1970. The independent preparatory school, which originated in Cavendish Square, hence its name, was founded by the Order of the Holy Child and is now run by an independent board of governors. Opposite,

the east side of the road is dominated by Top Rank Bingo, built into the rear of the old cinema on Parkway. Camden House (**No.199**), on the corner with Inverness Street, once a police station, is now a Camden Probation Service Hostel and Women's Resource Centre.

Arlington Road is crossed by **INVERNESS STREET**, the origin of whose name is unknown. There is a flourishing fruit and vegetable market, which is open every day except Sunday. **No.30** is the **Good Mixer** public house, rebuilt after bombing. West of the junction the row of terrace houses **Nos.40-44**, dating from the 1840s, has been restored and boasts original windows and ironwork balconies.

At the top of Inverness Street is delightful **GLOUCESTER CRESCENT**. It has the same source of name (the Gloucester Gate of Regent's Park) as Gloucester Avenue. Most of the houses date from around 1845-50, although three houses at the southern end existed before the 1840 sale of land by Lord Southampton. These are the present **Nos.1 and 2** and another, which stood on the petrol station site at the corner. The impressive Italianate terrace with towers, **Nos.3-22**, was designed by Henry Bassett (see section 4), who bought this plot at the 1840 sale. The houses opposite, of nicely linked design, appear to be by another hand. During the 1970s and 80s the

terrace attracted many residents from the world of the arts.

Back on **ARLINGTON ROAD**, the modern housing development on the corner with Inverness Street was constructed in 1994 by the Community Housing Association on the site of a large Camden Council Depot built in the early 1960s. An 1870 Ordnance Survey map shows an earlier use as a timber yard, probably belonging to Collard and Collard on nearby Oval Road. Part of the Camden Depot, **No.211**, remains in use as the base for Camden Community Transport. **EARLY MEWS** is shown on Daw's map of 1849 and is said to be named after Joseph Early, a plumber, who was a member of a family firm of builders based in Camden High Street. During the 1930s **Nos.8 and 9** Early Mews was the workshop of Pesaresi and Son and Spinelli, who made mechanical pianos.

The massive brick building with elaborate white porch on the east side of the road is **Arlington House**, formerly Rowton House. Designed by H B Measures and built in 1905, it was the last of a series of working men's hostels set up and financed by Lord Rowton, who was private secretary to Disraeli. In 1983 the building was purchased by Camden Council and managed by the UK Housing Trust. Refurbishment of the interior ended the old system of cubicles: two cubicles became one room and it now caters for 386 men. In 1993 the council sold the hostel to the Arlington

Nos.210 and 208 Camden High Street (west side) in the 1890s (?). See p 56

Housing Association, a charity set up to run it.

JAMESTOWN ROAD was originally divided into two parts, Upper James Street and Bolton Terrace. In 1884 the whole road became James Street, finally acquiring its present name in 1938. The derivation is uncertain: it may commemorate James Delancey, who gave his name to Delancey Street (p 65). The **Locomotive** public house has been at No.31 since at least 1856. It has a fine picture of a railway engine as its sign. Ahead, the **Recycling Centre** is at No. 28. It was opened in 1985 by the Greater London Council as the first ever of its kind in London, after the 1983 closure of the Camden Refuse Transfer Station, so called because the refuse was transferred to the canal onto which it backs. In 1993 it recycled 3218 tonnes of waste. In the 1890s stables of the London General Omnibus Company occupied this site.

Until the 1890s there were three canal wharves and basins to the north of the street. One of these, Bewley Cliff Wharf, was on the site of the striking glass-fronted building, **No.32 - Bewley House**, designed by Max Hutchinson (President of the RIBA 1989-91) for the J S Pathology Laboratories and opened in 1991.

On the site of **Gray's Auctions Rooms** at No.34 was another of the three wharves. It was here that William Leftwich established one of his Ice Wells in the mid-19th century. The *Pictorial Times* in 1846 described how the ice was collected from the canal by barges with sledge

The houses on p 54 in 1994.
No.208 is still a restaurant!

hammers at the bow. The lead-lined well contained 1000 tons of ice, which would then be sold by cart to local residents and shopkeepers in the days before refrigerators. **Nos.38-46** was Gilbey's distillery and bottling plant, erected in the 1890s, which we have seen from the towpath.

An opening off the south side at No.57 leads into the **ROTUNDA COURTYARD**, a collection of buildings behind the former piano manufacturers at The Rotunda (p 52). The buildings renovated between 1991 and 1994 once housed the saw mill, glue boiling room, and French polishing and veneering workshops. Of the row of terrace houses opposite the Gilbey factory, **Nos.67-84** were built during the 1840s and retain many of their original features and **Nos.61-65** were added when the buildings behind were renovated in recent times.

A short walk along the Canal towpath leads back to **CAMDEN HIGH STREET**, which joins Chalk Farm Road at the Canal Bridge. In 1801, according to Thompson's map of St Pancras, only fields made up the stretch between here and the site of the present Tube station. By 1834 the west side of the street had been constructed; the east side was completed over the next 15 years. Many of the buildings date from this period, as shown by the 1838 plaque on the east side of the street at **No.212**. Photographs of Nos.210

and 208 in the 1890s and 1994 are on pp 54 and 55.

In the 1990s the influence of the market is reflected in the shops: open-fronted boutiques and indoor markets selling leather jackets, boots, jewellery and posters compete for tourist attention. Larger-than-life model signs of leather jackets, giant boots and a motorcycle bursting through the wall above some of the shops serve to advertise their goods. The signs draw the eye to the flats above, many of which retain their original features.

Three pubs occupy the northern end of the High Street. The late-Victorian **Oxford Arms** stands on the corner with Jamestown Road opposite the **Elephant's Head** at No.224. Further south the **Buck's Head**, No.202, was once owned by Eliza Barrow whose husband murdered her by boiling up arsenical flypapers.

The St Pancras Street Directory of 1867 shows how different this road once was. Between the Elephant's Head and Buck's Head (originally Stucley Terrace) were a confectioner, china dealer, toy warehouse, cooper, grocer, tallow chandler and pawnbroker. Nowadays, further down the east side is the weekend outdoor market, selling a range of goods from handmade clothes to bootlegged music. No.184 is **The Electric Ballroom**. Once used for ballroom dancing, it now houses pop concerts in the evenings and market stalls during the day at weekends. In Kelly's

Post Office Directory for 1926-7 this address was listed as the offices for the Customs and Excise and the Ministry of Health Insurance's district inspector.

At No.211 on the west, past Inverness Street, was the **Plaza Cinema** (closed September 1994), a showcase since 1977 for foreign-language and art films. There had been a cinema here since c.1911, at one time called the Britannia Picture Palace. It was closed in 1994 to make way for development of the whole block, which will affect the market in many ways.

At the junction with Kentish Town Road is the **Underground station**, reputedly on the site of the original **Black Cap** pub (p 59). The inn was taken over by parish officers in 1778 as the second St Pancras workhouse, but it soon became overcrowded and, in 1809, it was moved to Pancras Road. In 1790 Brown's Dairy was established at the corner, being numbered 176 Camden High Street and 1 Kentish Town Road. The cows supplying the milk grazed in the fields in west Kentish Town until the 1840s. Fitted up handsomely with oak framework and costly embossed and engraved plate glass, the dairy became known as 'The Cows' Cathedral'. It was demolished about 1903 in connection with the building of the Underground Station, which opened in 1907. The station suffered bomb damage in WW II, but was repaired with the red tile facings originally specified by Leslie Green.

Camden Tube Station to Mornington Place

(see map 1 at end of book)

THE HIGH STREET south of the Underground station is the oldest part of Camden Town. In 1751 the only buildings in existence were the alehouses of Old Mother Red Cap and Old Mother Black Cap. Surrounded by fields, these 'Halfway Houses' afforded suitable places of refreshment between Tottenham Court and Hampstead.

Camden Town got its name from Charles Pratt, created first Earl of Camden in 1786, who held land to the east of what is now the High Street which he leased out in 1780 for 1400 houses. He took the name Camden from his residence in Chislehurst which had been named after William Camden, a 16th-century headmaster of Westminster School. Many of the local names stem from Charles Pratt, his family and associates, for instance Greenland Street after his builder Augustine Greenland. While the east side of the High Street was developed by Pratt, the west was held by Charles Fitzroy, Baron Southampton. The plots he leased were much smaller, and this is reflected in the narrower buildings noticeable to this day. It is also apparent that there were originally small gardens in front of the houses on the east side (between Greenland Street and Crowndale Road); as the street expanded, stalls developed into shops on the garden sites. The name High Street was designated only in 1863, when all the shops and houses on both sides were renumbered. What were built as homes are now workshops, offices and residential flats, in many cases in dire need of a facelift.

The houses in the residential streets, which developed 1820-40, were all built in similar style – three-storey, often with basement, half stuccoed with small ironwork balconies and a uniformity of fenestration, though some houses on Arlington Road have arched windows on the ground floor.

A major feature of the industrial life of this area was the manufacture of upright (and some grand) pianos. In 1911, 133 of the 136 piano manufacturers in Britain were based in London, 9 being south of the Thames and the rest spread across Islington and Camden. A host of associated suppliers of ivory keys, actions, hammers, felts and wires grew up around them. Names of note are Collard and Collard, Henry Ward, John Spencer, William Squire, George Rogers & Son, J J Hopkinson and Gunther & Horwood.

The walk begins at the five-way junction near the Underground Station. At the south-east corner stands **The World's End** pub. Until 1986 this was the Old Mother Red Cap which had a long and intriguing history dating back to England's Civil War. Rocque's map of St Pancras c.1746 refers to 'Old Mother Red Caps', but whether this implied two is not clear. Legend has it that it was named in the 17th century after Jinney, daughter of a Kentish Town brickmaker who had been a camp follower in Marlborough's army. Both her parents were hanged for witchcraft and Jinney herself was a suspect witch who came to be known as Mother Damnable. Three of her lovers came to bad ends. The first was hanged for sheep-stealing, the second disappeared and the third was found burnt to death in the oven of Jinney's cottage. She was accused of his murder but was acquitted when friends attested that the dead man used to hide in the oven to get away from her. Another sinister visitor was the 17th-century

Park Street & Mother Redcap, Camden Town.

highwaywoman Moll Cutpurse, and the highway robber John Fowler was shot dead nearby in 1708. Amongst gentler pursuits, there were tea gardens here alongside the 17th-century alehouse, popular until the 19th century for taking the fresh country air.

On the opposite side of the High Street the figure of Britannia, in a niche above **No.187** on the corner of Parkway, is all that remains of yet another High Street pub, called the Britannia, which closed its doors in 1962. Further south on the west side is the **Black Cap**, which has been at **No.171** since 1781 when (as the Mother Black Cap) it moved from the site of the Tube station. High on the front of the building is the black painted bust of the witch herself.

The east side as far as Pratt Street was called Camden Place until 1863. **No.158** has the date 1889 inscribed on a strip above the second floor, which shows the later age of this terrace. At **No.152** lived Martineau F Lance, hatter, who was also registrar of births and deaths for Camden Town (St Pancras street directory, 1867). On the side of the bank at **No.140** a more elaborate inscription, again dated 1889, features the initials JLB, which may have been those of the Joint London Bank.

Postcard of about 1910. Park Street is now Parkway and Mother Redcap The World's End (but still a pub).

Further down the east side can be seen the red brick gables of **Bowmans**. Once the most important furniture store in Camden Town, it dominated this side of the street. In 1864 Robert and Thomas Bowman, of Lakeland stock, set up an upholstery business at No.108. Thomas continued to extend the firm with mass-produced furniture for the growing middle class, aiming to be 'the complete house furnishers'. In 1900 the proprietors boldly announced that, following the relief of Mafeking, there would be an immediate migration of thousands from England to the Orange Free State and Transvaal and that they had 'gigantic preparations for the complete furnishing of homes of those migrating'. The gabled façade, with attractive mosaic decorations of a Viking ship, a steam engine and a list of furnishing wares, dates from 1893 after a fire destroyed part of the earlier premises. What remains is however only a fraction of what it was, as much of the building (Nos.124-112) was refurbished in the 1980s. The name Bowman survives on the High Street in a single outlet at **No.126**.

The Dalziel Brothers set up a fine-art books business in a small printing office at **No.100** in 1857 and under the Camden Press imprint built up a printing and publishing firm. Three of the brothers became noted wood engravers associated with the work of Pre-Raphaelites Millais and Rossetti, and also produced

illustrations for *Hard Times, Arabian Nights* and *Alice in Wonderland*. **No.161** was the premises of Horatio Webb, cheesemonger (plaque on the front: HW 1865; full name lettered on the side). Beside it is **UNDERHILL PASSAGE**, formerly Pleasant Passage, now leading to Marks & Spencer's car park. In the 1910s there was a Marks & Spencer bazaar at **No.133**, which had grown into a department store by 1939. Part of the present M&S site was once a cinema, the Electric Palladium.

Past **PLEASANT ROW**, which unlike the Passage retains its name, is an inscription above the shop at **No.135** to Sidney Bolsom, boot dealer, 1925. **Nos.125-133, Bedford House**, is (1994) home to a number of social service organisations including the London Ecology Unit, the Disability Resource Team and the London Housing Unit research team. Camden Council also base part of their social services here.

On the corner with Delancey Street is Woolworth's, which arrived in Camden in the 1930s. This site was previously the studio of the painter George Morland (1763-1804), who is buried in the churchyard of St James' Church (p 39). On the other side of Delancey Street is the **Bar Royale**, No.111, formerly the Brighton Arms, built by Thorpe and Furness in 1889. (They were also responsible for other pubs in the area and in 1895 had their offices at No.154.) Its decorated façade features reliefs of vividly coloured painted fruit and intriguing faces wearing beards and crowns.

At the junction with Mary Terrace (p 63), a modern building, **Nos.93-95**, fills the gap caused by the demolition of the Bedford Theatre (p 63) in 1969.

On the east side, the **Liberties Bar** at **No.100**, on the corner with Pratt Street, was called before 1989 the Camden Head. Beyond it **No.78** used to be Trills, the stationers and printers, locally a well-known family firm. Originally at No.131, the business was set up by Harold Trill in 1903 and closed in the 1980s. Both he and his son were to become mayors of Camden. 'Trills for Typewriters' is still (in 1994) visible in bold lettering on the front of No.78. **No.80** housed another stationer and printer, R&J Widdicombe, who established the St Pancras Gazette in 1866.

The modern supermarket at **No.74** is out of keeping with the style of the buildings on either side. In 1893 this was a registry office for servants, run by Sarah and Bessie Harris. From 1907 Miss Mary Stevens continued to run the registry alongside her tobacconist and stationer's business. Also associated with these premises were the headquarters of the 17th North Middlesex Rifle Volunteers, who became the 19th London Regiment in 1908 when the new drill hall was opened. During WW II this building was used for the distribution of ration books and gas masks and some local people still refer to it as 'the old 19th'.

At **No.52** is the hardware store opened by Frank Romany at the end of WW I. Although sold by the family in the 1980s, the name – and its reputation – continue into the 1990s. Francis Cowtan was a perambulator and invalid carriage maker at **No.50** as far back as 1874 and the firm still existed during WW I. Reputedly, the Camden Town branch of the Mormon Church met here in 1870. Next door, on the corner of Plender Street, is the mock-Tudor **Wheatsheaf** pub (No.48). There has been a pub of this name here from at least 1867. Also from around this date traded a furniture dealer, one Ephraim Rainbow, at **No.46**, and in 1907 these premises were taken over by the Star Furnishing Company. Note that on this stretch, above shop level, there is faded lettering which indicates other former uses such as 'Dining Rooms' at No.46 and 'Makers and Repairers - C. Morgan' at No.18.

On the west side of the street (previously called Southampton Row), **No.57** has *WB 1862* on the building; W Beard, fishmonger, is recorded as living here in 1867. The **Princess Beatrice** pub on the corner of Miller Street has stood here since at least 1864, when John Burnman was listed as wine and spirit merchant.

Until 1825 trees still shaded both sides of the southern end of the street, but a fire across the road in that year at Messrs Gunther & Horwood's, one of the many Camden Town piano factories, damaged them so badly that they had to be felled and were never replaced. Gunther's old building, behind the present **No.12**, was later used by another firm of piano manufacturers – Collard & Collard – after their premises in Oval Road had been destroyed by fire in 1851. By 1848 the building was in use as a place of worship for the congregation of Park Chapel (p 65), which had burnt down on 6 June that year in Arlington Road. Later it became a temporary church while St Matthew's, Oakley Square (demolished in 1977) was being built. In January 1850, No.12 became the home of the illustrious North London Collegiate School, where boys could obtain 'a sound commercial and classical education based on religious principles'. The school was still in existence here in 1897, after which the premises were used by Oetzmann & Co's cabinet factory until 1955. Part of the site was occupied by the Camden Town Library from 1964 to 1994.

Obliquely opposite at **No.33** is the jewellers J A Lake & Co, established 1868, and situated here since 1872. The shop has been beautifully restored to its 1915 appearance by the present owner. At **No.15** an iron plaque above a yard entrance is all that remains of Allworthy Bros, pawnbrokers; it shows a relief of the three gold balls and offers 'Money advanced on pictures, bronzes and violins etc with safes and fireproof rooms'. In 1994 fire damaged this sign so that it is only partly discernible. Other occupants included a shoemaker, a stay and crinoline maker, and a draper.

Up to 1866 an old toll house and bar stood in the road where the **Cobden Statue** now stands. A 19th-century account tells us that one of the 'pikemen' had been an amateur gardener who 'raised an embankment of road-drift to enclose the evidence of his taste for floricultural adornment'. When the toll-house and bar were removed their place was taken by the larger-than-life Sicilian marble statue of Richard Cobden, Liberal MP and 'Apostle of Free Trade'. This was put up in 1868, by public subscription, to honour the man who helped establish free trade between England and France. The project was largely financed by Napoleon III, the total cost being about £320. Sculpted by the brothers Wills of Euston Road, Cobden is seen in everyday dress of the period, holding a parliamentary roll, addressing the Mornington Crescent Tube station as if he were making a speech in the House of Commons. The statue bears the inscription 'Cobden, The Corn Laws Repealed, June 1846'. The unveiling ceremony was immortalised by Henry Dixon, photographer, of Albany Street, from the vantage point of a window opposite (see *Camden History Review 9*).

The reason for choosing this site for the monument remains unclear since Cobden was born in Dunford Farm, Midhurst, Sussex and was a cotton seller in Manchester before entering Parliament. The link between the Cobden name and the area was continued when in 1885 Cobden's second daughter Ellen, then aged 37, married the painter Sickert, who later lived in Mornington Crescent. She divorced him in 1899.

At the junction of the High Street with Crowndale Road stands what was once an elegant Edwardian playhouse, the **Camden Palace**, built around 1900 at a cost of £50,000. The architect was W G R Sprague, the man responsible for the design of numerous theatres in London and its suburbs. Messrs Waring & Gillow carried out the interior decoration in the then popular Louis XV style. (Under the influence of the then Prince of Wales it was fashionable to be francophile, even in unfashionable Camden Town.) The building, lit by electricity, had a seating capacity of over 3000, and featured a winter garden and promenade. Ellen Terry travelled from Brighton to open the theatre on 21 December 1900, and a pleasing copper bas-relief in the foyer commemorates the event. After WW I the building became a cinema, as did several other London theatres. Later it was used as radio and TV studios and since the 1970s asa restaurant and disco. Now a listed

building, the Camden Palace is a thriving night spot for the younger generation.

On the opposite side of the High Street is the **Southampton Arms**. The present building dates from the mid-19th century and retains outside the remains of the gas jets which were lit after dark to publicise the pub.

At the end of the High Street, on the right, is **MORNINGTON CRESCENT**, begun in 1821 and fully inhabited by 1832. It was named after the Earl of Mornington, Governor-General of India, eldest brother of the Duke of Wellington and a great friend of the Fitzroy family. Although now one of the saddest-looking streets in this area, evidence of its former elegance can still be seen in original features such as ironwork balconies, railings and windows. When first built, the houses overlooked neatly planted gardens, with fields to the east keeping at bay the dense development creeping up from the south. The backs of the house in the Crescent looked across fields to the recently built Park Village East and the newly named Regent's Park.

The first residents of the area were middle-class families, who usually installed servants on the top floor. Clarkson Stanfield (1793-1867), marine artist and friend of Charles Dickens, lived at **No.36** in 1832. Residents of the 1860s included two professors of music, a dental surgeon, a surveyor and a valuer. **No.12** was occupied by a seminary. By the end of the

19th century, however, the growth of the railway had lowered the status of the area and many of the houses were divided up into cheaper lodgings. In the 1920s the houses finally lost the central garden to a developer who built there the Carreras cigarette factory (p 41) and altered the Crescent for ever.

As a blue plaque attests, Walter Sickert (1860-1942) lived at **No.6**. Probably the most significant English impressionist painter of his day, he was a member of the Camden Town Group, formed at the beginning of the 1900s. They adopted the name as an expression of the spirit of the group, which found many of its subjects in 'the simple life of the lower and middle classes...so richly exemplified by that neighbourhood'. Spencer Frederick Gore (1874-1914) lived at **No.31** until 1912. He was the first president of the Group. Other members included Augustus John, Harold Gilman, Lucien Pissarro and J B Manson, one-time Director of the Tate Gallery, where the Group's work is well represented.

On the south corner is the double-sized granite **'Metropolitan Drinking Trough'**, a companion to one in Albany Street (p 25) and a gift in 1878 of Mrs Florence Upton-Cottrell-Dormer. The name Florence remains visible on the narrow end. At the corner with Arlington

Bedford Theatre programme (see p 63)

Road, **Mornington Court**, built in 1937, echoes the Egyptianising style of the Carreras factory (p 41).

ARLINGTON ROAD was named after Isabella Countess of Arlington, former holder of the lease of the Manor of Tottenham Court. Arlington Street, as the southern part was initially called, was developed on the east side (Nos.1-37) as early as 1806; there was nothing but a few

fields to the west until the Crown development of Regent's Park. Arlington Street west side was a nursery garden until 1839, but built over by 1840. The London and Birmingham Railway cut a swathe through the fields, and by the end of the 1840s streets were laid out right up to the railway. Many of the terraces of Arlington Road have been renovated, and provide a good example of the typical modest town

house of this period.

Arlington Road links the west ends of the passageways of humbler houses and workshops which lead off the High Street. **BEATTY STREET**, originally Nelson Street, in tribute to the Admiral's success at Trafalgar, was renamed in 1937. There are two possible derivations, both nautical: Sir William Beatty, who was Nelson's surgeon, and Admiral Lord Beatty, Commander-in-Chief in WW I, who had died in 1936. **CARLOW STREET** used to be Caroline Street, built in 1821, the year in which George IV's queen died. The name was changed in 1865 because too many London streets bore this name. An old warehouse there has been strikingly refurbished to house the building engineers Ove Arup. **MILLER STREET** was named after its builder John Miller, who built on this and surrounding streets from 1811 onwards.

In the early 1850s the poet and painter Dante Gabriel Rossetti lived at **No.38** with his brother William and sister Christina, themselves both poets, and his parents. Their father, an Italian political refugee, was a distinguished commentator on Dante and professor of Italian at King's College. Rossetti was a prominent member of the Pre-Raphaelite movement. He helped Frederick Denison Maurice found the Working Men's College (opened 1854). Charles Dibdin (1745-1814) at **No.34** wrote *Tom Bowling* as well as some 1400 songs and 30 dramatic pieces.

The flats on the east side of Arlington Road, a post-war development by St Pancras Council, replaced terrace houses like those opposite. **Fairfield** is on the site of St Matthew's School. The **lamp posts** in Arlington Road are good examples of early electric posts, with a flower and leaf decoration and the figure of the boy martyr St Pancras contained in a Greek-style frame.

Just to the north is **MARY TERRACE**, originally Mary's Terrace. A car park just beyond marks the site of the famous **Bedford Tavern**, originally No.1 Grove Place which became Grove Street and finally part of Arlington Road). Five of the original 10 houses of Grove Place are still standing, as **Nos.90-98** Arlington Road, with moulded Coadstone or stone heads over their doors. The Bedford Arms had a tea garden, with arbours and a well-kept bowling green; coffee as well as beer was served and there was a shrimp stall. Unlike public houses, tea gardens were respectable places where ladies could properly be seen on Sunday afternoons. On gala days there were balloon ascents. In July 1824, Mr Rossiter made an ascent from the Bedford in aid of the family left by Mr Harris, who had perished in a similar exploit. Mr Rossiter and his co-pilot set off at 5 pm, landing eventually at Havering Park in Essex. The Morning Chronicle reported that the two aeronauts were provided with a post-coach and returned at once, reaching the Bedford again at 10.30 that night for celebrations.

A music hall to the rear of the Bedford Arms was opened in 1861. Admission cost fourpence and each man was allowed two women guests free of charge. The music hall had its origins in public house entertainment and, in spite of its popularity, it was not considered a fit place for women and children. The music hall had restricted access from the High Street via a narrow alley which ran parallel to Mary Terrace. Only when Nos.93-95 High Street were demolished did it acquire the prominent 'baroque' façade befitting the **Bedford Theatre** which it became in 1889. It was last used as a playhouse in 1950; the final productions included Sir Donald Wolfit's *Othello* and *King Lear*. The list of famous players appearing at the Bedford before WW I is a lengthy one. In 1912 it included the 14-year-old Gracie Fields and Charlie Chaplin. Famous interiors of the theatre were painted by Walter Sickert.

On the corner with Delancey Street is the **Crown and Goose** pub, previously known as the Crown, done up and renamed in 1991. Past the renovated office block dated 1933 and a row of bay-fronted brick terraced houses, very different from the other residences in the street, is **UNDERHILL STREET**, which leads to the side entrance to Marks & Spencer in what was once Stanmore Place.

The **Mornington Sports and Leisure Centre** at **No.142-150** Arlington Road was once an electricity substation. Converted by Camden Council, it was opened to the public in 1982.

On the west side of the street the Catholic church of **Our Lady of Hal**, with an attractive mosaic over the porch, was opened in 1933. It had its origins in the Belgian religious order of Scheute, establishing a place of worship for Belgian exiles fleeing from WW I. Called Hal after a shrine near Brussels, the church was taken over and consecrated as a Catholic church in 1984. Further along on the same side it is amusing to come across, behind railings, a stationary red London double-decker bus, complete with model of its driver, being used as an estate agent's office.

If we now turn left up Parkway for a short distance we enter **ALBERT STREET** next on the left. The first of the terraced houses are the oldest in the street, built in 1840 without front gardens, unlike those further along. Generously wide, with an abundance of trees, Albert Street is the prettiest road in the area. At **No.19** William Sharp (1856-1905), author of *The Immortal Hour*, took a room 'where he could walk to work, yet sleep not far from birds and trees'. However, as a result of the noise and dirt from the railway on one side and the busy High Street on the other,

by the late 19th century many of the large houses in the area had fallen into multiple occupancy and remained so until the 1960s, when gentrification began. From 1969 this trend was fostered by the advent of improvement grants from the council and was nurtured by a traffic scheme which leaves Albert Street largely undisturbed. Since 1976, the **King's Fund Centre**, part of the King Edward's Hospital Fund for London (founded 1897), which promotes new ideas and practice in health and social services, has been based at **No.126**: it was built on the site of the Albert Optical Works, previously occupied by the Park Chapel Schools. A new development is planned for the east corner with Parkway.

At **No.65** lived the music critic Edward Holmes (1797-1859), friend of Keats, Shelley, Mendelssohn and Liszt. More recent residents have included the actor Denholm Elliot.

At the end of Albert Street is **MORNINGTON PLACE**, formerly Crescent Place. A short terrace of restored houses, **Nos.4-7**, next to the **Victoria** pub typifies the houses of the area. On the south side modern red brick council houses form part of a development that continues into **MORNINGTON TERRACE**. The 1849 map shows Mornington Road, as it was then, not with just a terrace on the east side but with quite grand semi-detached villas opposite.

They had a fairly short life; the map ominously labelled the land behind them 'acquired for railway'. The villas stood till 1900, but soon afterwards the North-Western Railway enlarged its cutting, leaving the terrace to face the noise and dirt of the tracks and decisively separating the area from the Park to which it had aspired. An illustration by J C Bourne in *The London and Birmingham Railway* of 1839 shows the *original* cutting being dug. **Nos.3-6** feature arched ground floor windows and attractive ironwork balconies. H G Wells lived from 1894 to 1898 at **No.12** with his mistress, Catherine Robbins, a former pupil. It was here that he wrote *The Time Traveller*, as *The Time Machine* was first called, *The Wonderful Visit* and *The Island of Dr Moreau*. At **No.20** lived Sir William Crookes (1832-1919), the famous scientist whose researches led to the use of X-rays. He was President of the Royal Society. Beyond the more recent blocks on either side of Mornington Street the long terrace (Nos.26-51), mostly restored, is of more lavish design, with pilasters dividing the houses vertically and railed balconies linking the whole. At **No.27** in the 1870s lived the barrister Count Richard Rainshaw, Marquess de Rothwell, who was responsible for Sharpleshall and Rothwell Streets (pp 75 & 77).

The **Edinboro Castle**, formerly 'Edinburgh Castle', pub at the northern end of Mornington Terrace once housed a free museum, a picture gallery and library, as well as tea gardens, where lawn billiards was a favourite pastime. In 1984 the pub was badly fire-damaged by an irate customer. When it reopened in 1987 it had been restored to its Victorian splendour by the brewers Charringtons.

The elegantly restored terraces at the top end of **DELANCEY STREET** (from which one can explore the walks in sections 1B or 4C) sweep down from the top of Parkway towards the High Street. Originally this part was named Stanhope Street and below Arlington Road it was Warren Street. The whole street was renamed in the 1840s after James Delancey of Marylebone, who was granted fields in the area by the Fitzroy family in 1795.

The poet Charlotte Mew, who was called by Hardy the best woman poet of her time, lived at what was once No.86 Delancey Street from 1922 to 1926. She committed suicide in 1928 after the death of her sister from cancer. The site became a car repair workshop at the junction with Parkway.

Through an arch on the north side of the street, beside **No.68**, a courtyard opens into a development of business premises with a mixture of new and old refurbished buildings. A little further on, a blue plaque informs us that Dylan Thomas lived briefly (1951-2) at **No.54**. It was a location he did not relish and described it as his London house of horror. A grade II-listed building, it was renovated in 1987 and converted into three flats. The gypsy caravan which stood in the garden in Thomas' day was restored at the same time.

On the south side, tucked away behind No.15, are the **Delancey Studios**, built on a derelict plaster works by Camden Council in 1981. The two-tiered quadrangle built of yellow brick at a cost of £237,000 accommodates 16 two-person flats.

On the corner with Arlington Road, where we have already noticed the Crown & Goose (p 63), flats have replaced the Park Congregational Chapel, with a school building behind it, victims of WW II bombing. The **Snooker Centre** was a public hall in the 1880s, an ice rink in 1903 and a cinema, The Dara, in 1908. In more recent times it was a bingo hall.

A short walk up the High Street brings us back to the Camden Town station.

Section 4 Between the railway and Primrose Hill

(see map 1 at end of book: this area is the northwest sector embraced by the mainline railway and Prince Albert Road)

THIS AREA forms the major part of the farm land sold by Lord Southampton in 1840 for residential development. The sale plan envisaged virtually universal coverage by semi-detached villas, but the coming of the railway changed that drastically.

Although villas were suitable for purchasers facing Regent's Park Road, sites approaching the dirt and noise of the railway could attract only poorer purchasers, for whom terraces of smaller houses were built, and long villa gardens gave way to small industries.

We describe the area in three walks, two of which start from the Chalk Farm Tube station, crossing the railway by the old 'Primrose Hill' railway station, and the third from the junction of Parkway with Gloucester Avenue, a 5-minute walk from Camden Town Tube station.

Rowlandson's view (1798) of the turnpike in Hampstead Road. On the left, St James's Chapel (see p 39), demolished in 1956

68 *Chalcot Square, unchanged since the late 1850s*

Chalk Farm station via Regent's Park Road to Chalcot Square

(see map 1 at end of book

CHALK FARM Underground station opened when the line to Hampstead was built in 1907. Regent's Park Road starts across the road from here and follows the line of the ancient lane to Lower Chalcot Farm, or Chalk Farm Tavern, which the railway from Euston cut through when it was built in 1837. At the junction, modern fast-food outlets front a new development on the site of the Adelaide Tavern where trams from Tottenham Court Road used to terminate, defeated by the steepness of the hill northwards (and also, possibly, by the Hampstead borough boundary); the trolleybuses that replaced them had a turning loop in the tavern forecourt. Pedestrians crossing the railway from this side also face a climb, but a short one, over the main-line railway bridge.

Just before the bridge a lane leads straight ahead to office/workshops which occupy a former hostel building for engine drivers whose tour of duty ended in London far from home. The station building on the bridge served platforms on the North London Railway (the 'local' railway linking Kew with the City, not the main line to Birmingham) at the station

which has been variously named Hampstead Road, Camden Town, Chalk Farm and Primrose Hill but closed in 1992. This station is dealt with in *The Streets of Belsize,* although it lies in fact on what was the St Pancras side of a shifting parish and borough boundary. The **bridge** itself is interesting. The first bridge was clearly brick-built, as can be seen in contemporary illustrations, but when it was demolished for railway widening in 1846 it was replaced in iron. The bridge was pedestrianised in 1972 and has borne several decorative paintings, the scheme visible in 1994 having been painted by local artist Andolye Luck.

Over the bridge, on the left-hand side is the **Pembroke Castle** public house, which invokes the former name (abolished in 1867) of a terrace at this end of the road. The intended street pattern was disturbed by an early expansion of the railway site, by which time a terrace of four pleasant villas had already been built by Henry Bassett (an architect described more fully in Section 4C) at this junction of Gloucester Avenue with Regent's Park Road. Two of the houses had to be pulled down almost as soon as they were built, to

accommodate the new road layout, and it is still possible to see evidence of this on the side of **No.196** Regent's Park Road at the junction. No.196 has frequently been a doctor's residence; its single-storey extension was built around 1890.

Before the early 1830s and the arrival of the London and Birmingham Railway, the lane to Chalk Farm Tavern had only three other houses on that north side – Bianca Lodge, Bow Cottage and Montrose House – which have all gone. Bianca Lodge was pulled down to make way for King Henry's Road to join Regent's Park Road in the 1860s. One of the houses built instead in 1854 was called Essex Villa and still exists as **No.111** Regent's Park Road.

On the northern corner site of **REGENT'S PARK ROAD** rose a group of buildings, **Nos.115-117**, which in 1865 formed the Boys' Home for the Training and Maintenance of Destitute Boys Not Convicted of Crime. The Home had previously been known as The Boys' Home for the Maintenance by their own Labour of Destitute Boys not Convicted of Crime; it moved here from 44 Euston Road, when the original building had to give way to the extension of the Midland Railway line to St

Pancras. The Home had been founded in 1858 by two philanthropists, both named George Bell though unrelated, one resident in Albert (now Prince Albert) Road and the other in Hampstead. The Home moved to three houses on the Regent's Park Road site in 1865, and more houses were added over the next 20 years. The boys attended the new St Mary's, Primrose Hill from 1872 until 1889, after which they had their own chapel. The Home sheltered over 1000 destitute boys over 60 years, training them in various occupations including the playing of band instruments, considered useful if they joined the armed services. They were a feature of the district, marching with their band to Primrose Hill, where they exercised and played football matches (see *Camden History Reviews 2,18*). The Home was closed in 1920.

Bow Cottage, one of the original houses in the lane, was incorporated in the Home and became its Infirmary. Essex Villa became the superintendent's house in the 1880s. The Chapel, now **No.109a**, built around 1872, is in 1994 used as commercial premises and has had an intermediate floor inserted. Bow Cottage became a mere shell after a fire in 1972 and is now demolished. Its circular front garden, which boasted a fountain, became the main yard of the Home. This area is now fronted by a wine shop; its previous use as a petrol station is still evident from

the pediment. In 1982 the main buildings were heightened and given extra windows to house a block of flats, which was later extended along King Henry's Road over the Boys' Home yard.

Nos.192-184 and **Nos.182-174**, built in the late 1840s and early 1850s, are terraces of large houses with basements, known as Northumberland Terrace. The plot on which these houses stand was bought at the 1840 Southampton Estate sale by Thomas Pocock, whose brother Lewis married Eliza Bassett, Henry's sister. Thomas and Lewis were cousins of John Thomas Pocock, the diarist (see *Diary of a London Schoolboy 1826-1830*). These houses have always been residential and have mostly been converted into flats.

On the opposite side, the shops at **Nos.109-91** form a terrace with dwellings of three floors above them. The block was built in the early 1870s in nearly symmetrical form, with a very shallow pediment in the centre but with non-matching end houses, although these are similar in the use of circular-headed windows on the second floors. From the start there was a wide variety of shops here. **No.109** was a bakery for most of its life, became the local public library in the 1950s and was recently an antique shop owned by Ron Weldon, husband of the novelist Fay. **No.105** was the local post office with chemist attached and by 1884 had a dentist on the premises as well.

The post office moved by the turn of the century to **No.162** on the opposite side of the road; later, back in the old terrace as **No.91**, on the corner with Erskine Road, it is the centre of Kingsley Amis's novel *The Folk who Live on the Hill* (1990). For many years No.91 was a china and glass warehouse, and later a laundry. **No.95** remained a dairy for many years, while **No.97** started life as a meat warehouse. **No.99** was first a draper's and by 1884 a fruiterer's. In the 20th century it became a tailor's shop; by WW II it was a doctor's surgery and has remained so.

ERSKINE ROAD makes its appearance in maps and directories around 1868. The road was named after Lord Erskine (1750-1823), whose most important local residence was Erskine House, adjoining the Spaniards Inn in Hampstead. He became Lord Chancellor, 1st Baron Erskine in 1806. The old St Pancras boundary cut across Erskine Road between No.1 and the Chalk Farm Tavern, so the greater part was originally in the Eton Estate in Hampstead. The St Pancras part of the road lies on what was once the Chalk Farm Tavern site, bought by the LNWR to allow the Eton Estate an outlet into Regent's Park Road. The 1874 Directory gives four houses on the southern side – **No.1** occupied by a milliner and a sweep, **No.2** by coffee rooms, **No.3** by a rag dealer and **No.4** by a Mr James Green.

ERSKINE MEWS is not mentioned

until 1884, when it contains the usual stables, run by George Chapel, firewood manufacturers. Today the mews houses are rebuilt and modernised and form a charming enclave, reached by an archway from Erskine Road.

Most of the north side of Erskine Road was occupied by Hindley & Sons, cabinet makers, until at least 1892. The building was then used by John Malcolm & Co,

Reed Organ Manufacturers, together with its large yard behind the shops in Regent's Park Road. Montrose House, one of the three original houses on Chalk Farm Lane, remained for some time as one of the outbuildings in the yard. Also off this yard may have been the temporary iron church, erected in 1867, housing the congregation who awaited the building of St Mary's, Primrose Hill, in 1872. The exact site of

the temporary church has not been located but it was perhaps reached by Erskine Road, down the side of the cabinet makers. In the Directories of 1868-72, its address is given as Ainger Road, Chalk Farm, and the only likely-looking building on the 1870 map is beside the yard. On 14 August 1906 Malcolm's Organ Factory burnt down, the blaze being sufficiently serious to merit mention in the St Pancras Book of Dates. The building that replaced it is now occupied by several smaller firms.

On the corner of Erskine Road with Regent's Park Road is a restaurant occupying the rest of the site of the **Chalk Farm Tavern**. The area behind, which previously was the tavern yard, is (1994) a firm of specialist auto-engineers. The present premises were built in 1853-4. (A short history is given in *Camden History Review 6*.) The first reference to a tavern here was in 1678, when a missing magistrate, Sir Edmund Berry Godfrey, was found murdered in a ditch at the foot of Primrose Hill: his body was found by two tradesmen and taken to the 'White House', a very modest inn at the time, which later became Chalk Farm.

The first innkeeper recorded in the Middlesex Licensing Records is Joshua Deane at Chalk House Farm in 1732. By 1800, the tavern had a long room and gardens and was a popular place to visit, although somewhat notorious for rough sports and, in particular, for duels fought

The Lemonia Restaurant on the site of the Chalk Farm Tavern, 1994

nearby on the hill. In the Napoleonic Wars, various regiments of Volunteers used the grounds for shooting practice. When the Primrose Hill railway tunnel was being built in the 1830s, the tavern was usually the first resting place of unfortunate navvies killed in the works.

When Lord Southampton decided to sell his land in this area in 1840, he put up Chalk Farm and its pleasure gardens as one lot, despite their being separated by the new Regent's Park Road. The gardens were a focal point from the 18th century until 1865. At the height of their fame, they boasted a bandstand known as a Chinese Orchestra, which was 36 feet high, and a dance floor capable of taking one thousand persons. By the mid-1860s, however, the brewers (Calverts) had sold off the garden for building plots and the Chalk Farm Tavern became just one of the many pubs in the area. In more recent times it has again become a highly fashionable venue. It is hard nowadays to visualise the pleasure gardens which once lay in front of the tavern. The shape is still there – a roughly semi-circular area, bounded by Berkley Road, Chalcot Square and Sharpleshall Street. Let us cross the road and explore Berkley Road.

BERKLEY ROAD, often spelt as Berkeley Road on old maps, marked the

Anonymous sketch of Chalk Farm Tavern, 1830

northern boundary of the old pleasure gardens and as such was present, though unnamed and without houses, in the parish map of 1849. The 1860 map shows the road clearly named. The name seems to have no local significance and may be just an attempt to achieve Mayfair elegance. Its first houses (on the left) were known as Norfolk Terrace. Opposite these nicely proportioned 1860s houses there is a medley of buildings. **Nos.2 and 4** were rebuilt in the 1980s in the style of the northern terrace, replacing an 'arterial-

road' style house with garage erected after bombing in WW II and curiously attached to **No.6**, a tall Victorian house which survived the bombing. It is in Tudor-Gothic style, as was, presumably, the whole original southern terrace. Next comes the **Chalk Farm Baptist Church**. The foundation stone was laid on 13 June 1870 and it was opened on 15 February 1871, with a capacity of 850 seats. The building was reconstructed in 1957 after bomb damage and under the foundation stone was found a bottle containing a copy of the *Camden & Kentish Town Gazette*, forerunner of the *North London Press*. **No.8**, beyond the opening into Eglon Mews, was a small organ factory, owned in 1884 by H T Widlake, Organ Builder. Rintoul Bros, Piano Makers, occupied it from 1911 to 1935, and from 1935 to 1960 Lambert of London manufactured pianos there. The building currently houses design consultants.

EGLON MEWS opens into Berkley Road at the side of the Baptist church. Its construction was proposed in 1867 by a Mr Berrill. (Was his first name Eglon, or did he invent this rather odd name?) The buildings are now modernised and form houses **Nos.1-7**. The 1870 Ordnance Survey map shows the central space occupied by stables. By 1900, the stables had been converted to a motor car works.

BERKLEY GROVE is at the end of Berkley Road on the left, between erstwhile

Norfolk Terrace (**Nos.1-9** Berkley Road) and the backs of houses in Chalcot Square. It contains various small businesses, some grouped around a former stable yard. Goad's Insurance Map of 1900 records the Endolithic Ivory Marble Company here, with a builder, J Sell & Son, on the right-hand side. The Grove seems to have been commercial from the first.

Following Berkley Road round to the right, we encounter some neo-Gothic houses marking the southern boundary of the old Tavern Gardens which despite being built many years later were eventually numbered (**34-39**) as part of **CHALCOT SQUARE** – one of the more irregularly shaped 'squares' in London. St George's Square, as it was known for almost a century, was laid out in the late 1850s. **Nos.1-10** appear in the 1858 Directory. The name was changed to Chalcot Square in 1937 in the LCC drive to eliminate duplicate names throughout London. Why it was originally called St George's Square remains a mystery. Bounded on three sides by tall terraced houses of distinguished, somewhat Flemish appearance, the Square is one of the most charming features of the district. The Square has a small public garden, with some acacias – fashionable trees in the 1850s. Opposite, **Nos.8-11**, which could almost be considered part of Chalcot Road, are among the oldest houses in the neighbourhood, appearing on the 1849 Parish Map before any others in the road.

Amongst the neo-Gothic houses is an interesting one, **No.36, "Turner House"**. Before WW II and until 1950, it was a hostel for blind women in the care of the Church Army. On Sunday, 22 September 1940, the Communion Service of St Mark's Church was held in the chapel of Turner House, because the church had been seriously damaged in an air raid the night before. In front of these houses bollards have been erected to impede the passage of cars between Chalcot Road and Regent's Park Road. Their ugliness is mitigated by some rather nice cobbled paving.

Residents of the Square appear to have been respectable rather than famous, though in later years it has attracted a fair share of those working in the media. In 1874, **No.1** was occupied by a Dr Read, who moved here from Rothwell Street around the corner. His younger daughter, Ethel E Read Mumford, gives an interesting account of life in this Square at the time in *Through Rose Coloured Spectacles*. The house was large enough for a surgery and consulting room as well as the family of five children and an appropriate number of servants. The doctor and his wife took in boarders – 'high class Japanese who were occasionally sent over by their Government to study in England'. Later, a mental patient, plus his male nurse, was found to be even more satisfactory financially and added less to the work of the house. Mrs Read Mumford recalls walking to the North London Collegiate School for Girls in Sandall Road, off Camden Road, and gives a vivid picture of the Chalk Farm scene in her day.

F J Furnivall, who lived at **No.3** St George's Square in the early 1880s, founded the Shakespearian Society and was a specialist in medieval English literature. **No.6** was a School for Ladies and may have been the Dame School referred to by Mrs Read Mumford when recalling her early school days.

The south-eastern exit from Chalcot Square is broad and contains a terrace of large houses on each side. Once Alma Terrace, the street became St George's Road in 1874 and **CHALCOT ROAD** in 1937. It continues from this exit with terraces of smaller houses, but is still of considerable width. At the cross-roads with Fitzroy Road, which is also of generous width, there is the **Princess of Wales** public house, presumably so named at the wedding of Princess Alexandra with the future Edward VII in 1863, about the time this area was developed.

Turning left into **FITZROY ROAD**, we encounter some pleasant terraces. Beside **No.8** is an entrance to an extensive back area, formerly and currently occupied by trade. It is not named as a definite mews. In 1874 Scrivener & White, a building firm, used this area. They built the 1870 showrooms of the Piano Factory at the other end of Fitzroy Road.

On the other side of the road, **Nos.1** and **3** form a pair of very attractive semi-detached villas. In 1847-62, No.1 was occupied by the developer Joseph Gandar (see also p 80), a prominent Muggletonian, ie a member of a religious sect founded in Commonwealth times. The pair were the first houses built on this plot and also the first houses in Fitzroy Road, which suggests that they were both built by Gandar. Originally these houses had very long gardens at the back, but the map of 1900 shows the end of the back of No.1 sold to a piano factory, J Spencer & Co, which reached into it from the end of Egbert Street. There is an artist's studio clearly visible on the map in the remaining garden of No.1 and in the 1904 Directory the resident is recorded as Willis Ward, artist. In fact the studio may well have been converted from a chapel built by Gandar for the Muggletonians. **No.3** retained its long garden for a time.

Fitzroy Road enters **GLOUCESTER AVENUE** opposite the inelegantly named **DUMPTON PLACE**, which has no street sign, and is a small cul-de-sac bordering on the railway. Known until 1872 as Fitzroy Place, it seems to have been used mainly for commercial purposes from the outset. The carriers Pickfords had a depot there for many years and are recorded in the 1880s and into the 1900s; it had a fish-curing works in the 1950s and now is a Volvo service centre. Below the wall at the end of Dumpton Place are the remains of steps which originally led to engine sheds.

In order to regain our starting point at Chalk Farm station we shall proceed up this northernmost stretch of Gloucester Avenue (in 1867 named Gloucester Road North) to the junction with Regent's Park Road and Bridge Approach. Other stretches of Gloucester Avenue (which was until 1937 three differently named roads) are described in sections 4B and 4C.

On the northern corner of Dumpton Place is the **Lansdowne** public house. The first Marquess of Lansdowne was William Petty, created Marquess in 1784, after successful negotiation of peace terms with the USA. He is commemorated in Mayfair and Bloomsbury streets as well; his connection with the Chalk Farm area is not clear. The three pubs on Gloucester Avenue – the Engineer, Lansdowne and Pembroke Castle – were built primarily for thirsty engine drivers and other railway employees. In the days of steam locomotives soot and grime were so much in evidence behind the houses on the east side that washing hung out to dry was immediately covered in black spots. Local housewives petitioned the Queen on the subject in 1958.

The 1874 Street Directory shows the upper end of Gloucester Avenue housing coffee rooms, a plumber, carpenter, bootmaker, tobacconist and grocer in one row. In 1884 **No.110** was occupied by C J Coxhead, Pianoforte Manufacturers, probably as a showroom. There is no sign of any of these now; the trim house-fronts have been reconverted to domestic use. However, part of the back gardens of many of the houses on the railway side are occupied by old railway-connected workshops, now discreetly converted into modern units for small businesses approached via passageways beside **Nos.122** and **134**. Pembroke Yard, which used to connect the passageways behind Nos.122-134, has been completely blocked off and has disappeared as a name. The odd-numbered houses across the street have neat front gardens, somehow invoking images of uniformed nursemaids and muffin men on foggy afternoons.

At the northernmost corner of Gloucester Avenue, where it meets the footbridge over the railway, we reach the **Pembroke Castle** again.

Section 4B
Old Tavern Gardens to Princess Road

(see map 1 at end of book)

AS IN THE PREVIOUS SECTION (4A), this exploration can begin at Chalk Farm Underground station, but it picks up the trail at the former Chalk Farm Tavern (now a Greek restaurant) in Regent's Park Road, at the point where we turned into Berkley Road.

Opposite the restaurant we see a terrace of shops, **Nos.172–146**, which were built in the late 1860s on the former tavern gardens. No.172 was originally a cheesemonger's and so has changed little, as it is now (1994) a grocer's. No.166 started life as a house agent's, Ekins & Broderick, and has returned to this use in recent years. No.158 was a butcher's continuously until the 1970s. No.156 is recorded in the 1874 Directory as Henry A Lovell, oil and colourman. Today this would be called a hardware store, so this shop has retained its original function throughout its existence. No.152 was originally a builder's, but by 1904 had become Yeomans, fruiterer, and this continues to be its shop sign. No.146 remained a pharmacist until the early 1990s.

SHARPLESHALL STREET marks the southern boundary of the former gardens at their junction with the Chalk Farm Tavern's shooting ground, which stretched towards Primrose Hill. The street was built in 1862 by Count Richard Rainshaw, Marquess de Rothwell, who named it after his home in Lancashire, Sharples Hall at Bolton le Moors. Richard Rainshaw Rothwell (1808–90), a barrister, was given his unlikely sounding title in 1860 by the King of Italy (see also Rothwell Street). Original 1862 houses remain on the southern side of the street but in 1961 the northern side was largely reconstructed to include a branch of Camden Libraries, which replaced a terrace of shops with dwellings over. Clearly, houses on the other side likewise had shops on the ground floor, which were listed in the 1872 Directory as a fruiterer, dyer, house decorator, haberdasher and saddler at **Nos.1,2,4,5** and 7. The original shop fronts were later replaced by domestic front doors and windows. Behind these houses **PRIMROSE MEWS**, formerly Sharpleshall Mews, is shown on all earlier maps as livery stables with living quarters above: it is now occupied by design studios which displaced a small billiard-table factory when it moved to more spacious premises.

Back in **Regent's Park Road**, the shops on the west side, south of the Tavern, **Nos.87-69**, of the early 1850s, do not form a uniform terrace: the line is broken by the curious 'cottage' look of **No.75**. This was originally the Primrose Tavern, built in 1846 in its own grounds before the other houses came, but by 1853 it was occupied by George Camp, Cow Keeper and Dairyman. By 1865 it was run by Mrs Mary Camp, presumably his widow, and it remained a dairy until 1904, probably without cows after 1870, when livestock was prohibited. The old cowshed still exists in the back yard. **No.83** was in 1867 a haberdashery, run by Mrs Mary Camp. This surely must be the ex-cowkeeper and dairy widow, adopting a new trade in the newly-built house. Later it became Cornelius Grimes, Juvenile Outfitters, which had moved across the road by 1884 to **No.136**. By 1993 it had become a restaurant, with a well-established vine growing inside the front window and emerging to swathe the little balcony above it. **No.77** started out as a builder's and became an undertaker's, Henney & Co, and in the space behind, hearses and horses could have been accommodated. This space, and the narrow opening leading to it between Nos. 75 and 77, became **MAYFAIR MEWS** in the early 1990s.

CHAMBERLAIN STREET is a cul-de-sac off Regent's Park Road, the blunt end of the street being on the old St Pancras borough boundary. Built in the mid-1850s, the original name was Bernard Street; this changed to Chamberlain Street in 1885. *London Street Names* suggests that the name commemorates a James Bradley Chamberlain, an optician in High Holborn admitted as a tenant of the Manor of Tottenham Court in respect of some land near Chalk Farm in 1860. The street is so symmetrical that it must represent the work of one builder. The houses are adorned with iron railings and cast-iron decorative windowbox holders, as well as the porch columns of the period.

Further along the west side of Regent's Park Road, the skyline is lower than that of the terraces opposite. **Nos.67-49**, dating from the early 1850s, have had varied careers, but **No.57** has been a fried fish shop for at least 50 years. This shop was first a stationer's and about 1900 became a bicycle shop. A garage long occupied **Nos.59-61**, partly on the site of old Chester Cottage, but this has now been displaced by a small supermarket. Its storage space behind was once the long gardens of these houses. The arch into **St GEORGE'S MEWS** is capped by two storeys of living accommodation at **No.53**. The first recorded occupant of St George's Mews was J Sell, carpenter, in 1854 – perhaps the founder of the builders in Berkley Grove. Later that year the Mews must have been a hive of industry, housing a smithy, a farrier, a builder, two chimney-sweeps and two cab owners. As **No.1** was a forge (of which no sign remains) and **No.63 Regent's Park Road** a harness and saddle maker, this made a useful enclave of associated trades. By 1904 only the smithy and one farrier remained. The workshops and stables on the south side have now been converted into houses.

Back in Regent's Park Road and passing one of the decorative St Pancras lamp standards in fairly good shape, we find **The Queens** public house, opened in 1854/5. Its inn sign has Queen Victoria on the park side and the young Queen Alexandra on the reverse. Built in more elaborate style than most pubs in the area, to match **St GEORGE'S TERRACE**, it opened in 1854/5.

The Terrace looks across Primrose Hill Road onto the green acres of Primrose Hill park and consists of imposing houses of three floors plus a basement, with their own private road and strip of communal gardens in front. The Terrace was built in the early 1850s in a style grander than its neighbours. The widow of Lord Byron is said to have died in one of the houses in 1860: the Directory of that year shows her occupying **Nos.10** and 11.

Of **PRIMROSE HILL ROAD**, only the short length from Ainger Road to Regent's Park Road lies in our area. The road was started at the north end in the 1860s, but it did not cut through to Regent's Park Road until the late 1870s. The block of flats called **Hill View** is on the site of the home for many years of two popular actors, Fred Terry (brother of Ellen Terry) and Julia Neilson, his wife and partner. For the first quarter of the 20th century the couple starred together in romantic costume dramas, the best remembered being *The Scarlet Pimpernel*.

Back on the other side of Regent's Park Road, the last terrace of shops with three storeys above forms **Nos.142-126**, built in the early 1870s. These have nice proportions, with a balcony railing and some unusual plaster ornamentation (fake arches, with 'impost' decoration in the form of many different kinds of leaf) over the first-floor windows. **No.142** has remained a wine and spirit merchant's since it first opened. **No.134** started life as a Ladies' Outfitters, turned to plumbing in the 1890s and, after many changes, became Primrose Hill Books, selling books old and new and Camden History publications. Miss Finlay at **No.130** is in the 1874 Directory as an ostrich feather manufacturer but, by 1884, she is merely a dyer and cleaner. **No.128** began as premises for a pianoforte manufacturer, George Youatt, but this can only have been showrooms or a components factory as there is hardly room for any serious piano building. For many years **No.126** was a dairy, first belonging to W Newman, who also had premises in Albany Street; it later housed a branch of United Dairies.

The GLC plaque on **No.122** marks the home from 1870 to 1894 of Friedrich Engels, political philosopher and friend of Karl Marx, living a short walk away in Maitland Park Road. Mary Burns, his common-law Irish wife, died in 1863 and he then lived similarly with her sister Lydia until 1878, when he married her by special licence on her deathbed. Engels died in 1896, not in his own house but in that of a friend, Ludwig Friedburger, Pathologist to the LCC, who lived at No.41 Regent's Park Road. **No.118**, on the corner of Rothwell Street, was the last London home of Count Richard Rainshaw, Marquess de Rothwell.

ROTHWELL STREET is narrow, with terraces of pretty, classical houses on each side, obviously the work of one builder. The site was purchased about 1861 by Rothwell, his address being given as Mornington Road (see Mornington Terrace) as well as Sharples Hall (see Sharpleshall Street). Further along Regent's Park Road are further terraces of elegant houses facing Primrose Hill. Two groups of four flanking Chalcot Crescent, **Nos.110–96**, were originally known as Queen's Terrace and built in the early 1850s. In **No.110** lived Thomas R Way until his death in 1913. He was a lithographer of some note, who produced and illustrated books on old London buildings and had assisted his father as lithographer to Whistler.

Contemporary with Queen's Terrace is the straight part of **CHALCOT CRESCENT**, whose attractive houses are graced with nice porches, rather like large sentry boxes. This part was originally called Chalcot Terrace and the curved part, built later in a slightly different style, was the first Chalcot Crescent: its houses on the east side have porches of Doric columns with balconies over. The street was generally residential from the date of building although in 1884 **No.7** was occupied by a teacher of languages, **No.42** by a glass stainer and **No.44** by a dressmaker. The 1904 Directory has a Baptist minister living at **No.2**. Presumably he was minister of the church in nearby Berkley Road. **No.3** was occupied at this time by a waterworks firm of Turncocks, listed as Joseph Selway and George Adams. **No.37** has a GLC blue plaque, put up in 1983 to commemorate a Dr José Rizal, who lodged there in 1888. He came to England 'to rescue, from the archives of the British Museum, the lost history of the Filipinos'. His work led to the Philippine Revolution in 1896 and he became a national hero.

Back in Regent's Park Road, **Nos.102-96** form the other half of what was Queen's Terrace. From here to the corner of Fitzroy Road stretches the large **Oldfield Estate**, comprising flats for the elderly. They replaced another long terrace, Nos.94-72, once called Regent's Park Gardens, and a large area behind, Regent's Park Gardens Mews, on a plot purchased by a Mr Oldfield in the 1840 sale. The terrace was demolished in 1963, together with the mews and the nearest pair of houses in Fitzroy Road. At No.90 lived 'Henry Handel Richardson', the pen name of Ethel Florence Robertson (1870-1946), an Australian novelist and translator. She lived in England from 1895: her novel, *The Getting of Wisdom* (1910), was turned into a successful and sensitive Australian film. At No.76 lived John Hayward Hawkins, a collector of antiquities and possessor of the 8th-century Witham Bowl. This priceless piece of Anglo-Saxon metalwork, known only from beautiful drawings held by the Society of Antiquaries, has never been traced since his death in 1877.

FITZROY ROAD is a straight, wide road with most of its original buildings, dating from 1850-80. In 1874 **No.54** was the home of the Rev William Galloway, the first Vicar of St Mark's (p 84). He was appointed Curate-in-Charge of the temporary church in 1849 and finally retired in 1888. From 1889 to 1891, H G Wells boarded with his aunt at **No.46**, while he was assistant master at Henley House School, Kilburn (see *The Streets of West Hampstead*). Significantly, he had the last of the Martian visitors in *The War of the Worlds* (1896) landing on Primrose Hill. The imposing **No.44** is the old Hopkinson pianoforte works, built in 1867. In her book, *A Land*, Jacquetta Hawkes, who lived at **No.39** in the 1950s, describes Hopkinson's as 'a lofty pedimented building in a subdued Roman style'. The building was later used as a factory for electric light fittings. At one time it was threatened with demolition but it has now been incorporated into a scheme for flats and houses which encompasses **Nos.38-50**. The Camden History Society carried out a survey of the old works building before conversion began. The factory covered a large area, extending behind the houses fronting on Fitzroy Road. Its architect was J T Christopher. Goad's Insurance Map of 1900 shows where the various processes were carried on. **No.44a**, the smaller building on the left, was built as showrooms in 1870.

Next to No.38 a wide passage, **HOPKINSON'S PLACE**, leads to a tree-shaded area beside the new Primrose Hill Community Centre, one of the most pleasing outcomes of the public protest against the demolition of the factory and its outbuildings: the Centre is housed in the original machine shop.

No.54 was the home of Professor J B S Haldane and his wife Charlotte – he a noted pacifist and expert on gas warfare and she a St Pancras Labour Councillor. Both were members, overt and covert respectively, of the Communist Party, meetings of which were frequently held at this address.

Across the road is a pair of large villas, **Nos.55** and 57. The 1884-85 Directory shows an artist living in each of these houses. Another artist, Michael Ayrton, was living at No.57 in 1964. In the centre of this end of the road is an odd-looking **electricity sub-station**, built at the turn of the century. At first glance it resembles nothing as much as an underground public convenience.

The terrace beyond the junction with Kingstown Street (p 79), **Nos.31-49**, is split in the middle by a narrow lane leading to the celebrated **PRIMROSE HILL STUDIOS**, originally protected by a gate which was locked at night. The plot containing the terrace and studios had been bought at the 1840 sale by H W Burgess, who also bought the Chalcot Square plot, but it was left untouched until the late 1870s, when it was acquired and developed by Alfred Healey, a local builder, who may have been his own architect. Built between 1870 and 1882, the studios are low, cottage-type buildings with artists' skylights, arranged around a rectangular courtyard. Many famous artists and musicians are associated with this delightful cul-de-sac. A wooden plaque on the wall gives a list of some notable residents, including Sir Henry Wood, Arthur Rackham and his wife Edyth, who was also an artist, J W Waterhouse, William Logsdale (correctly Logsdail) and Joseph Wolfe, a Victorian trio who were well-known painters in their time (Waterhouse's *Lady of Shalott* is in the Tate Gallery). Joseph Wolfe, described as 'Animal Painter and Naturalist', drew for the Zoological Society and moved here from Fulham to be nearer to his subjects. At the foot of the plaque is written: 'These studios appear in Joseph Hatton's novel *By Order of the Czar*.'

The Rackhams lived at **No.6** and this studio was occupied after 1939 by Lord Methuen, painter and trustee of the National Gallery and the Tate Gallery, who died in 1972. During WW II, Lord Methuen painted a picture of the piano factory in Fitzroy Road. Sir Henry Wood, founder of the Promenade Concerts, lived in **No.5**. In later years, residents have included Martita Hunt, the actress, and Margaret Webster, actress, director and writer. *A View from Primrose Hill* by Caroline Ramsden (Hutchinson Benham, 1984) gives an account of life in and around the Studios from 1935 onwards.

Continuing eastwards, we come to an

1850s terrace. Next to **No.29** is the entrance to **FITZROY YARD**. Originally a mews and then garages, the latter was later imaginatively converted to studios, offices and living quarters. At **No.23** Fitzroy Road a blue plaque records the fact that William Butler Yeats lived here as a small boy with his family before they returned to Ireland. Much more recently, in the 1960s, one of the flats in the house was the home of the tragic American poet, Sylvia Plath, who committed suicide there.

At the junction with Chalcot Road we turn right beside the first terrace which contains some shops. Between **MANLEY STREET** (once Egbert Terrace) and **CALVERT STREET**, the terrace has been rehabilitated by a housing trust as a series of houses and flats, the rear side having been completely rebuilt. The terraces on the northern side of Chalcot Road are intersected by **EGBERT STREET** (once Robert Street), a cul-de-sac built in 1865, and **EDIS STREET** (Eton Street until 1937), built some years earlier. Across the end of Egbert Street and behind the houses of Chalcot Road up to Edis Street is an old piano factory, now split into multiple workshop units with a high proportion of distinguished architectural firms. The approach at **No.7** Chalcot Road sports the name Utopia Village.

The original development in this area was by Messrs Manley and Rogers, whose works were in Chalcot Road, and it is possible that one of the builders was an Egbert and the other a Robert. The Eton name may have been associated with the nearby Eton Estate, although we are now in the Southampton Estate; Colonel Sir Robert Edis (1839-1927) was an LCC councillor and an architect. (For more about Edis, see *Camden History Review 7*.) Calvert Street commemorates the owners of land in this area and in particular the brewery by the Gloucester Avenue canal bridge (p 80).

Manley Street leads to what was an area of Railway Cottages owned by the railway company. There were three streets running roughly parallel to Chalcot Road, named Egbert Place, Manley Street and Kingstown Street. Most of the railway cottages were demolished in 1970, to be replaced not by the then-fashionable tower block desert but by the houses and flats of **AUDEN PLACE**, arranged around a courtyard. A housing trust development, it was named – with no evident local connection – for the poet W H Auden, soon after his death.

At either end of the new development, the disjointed ends of **KINGSTOWN STREET** (Fitzroy Place until 1872) contain houses either built, or rebuilt, since WW II. The boundary wall between the Auden Place development and the gardens of houses in Regent's Park Road still bears traces of the back yard buildings of the old railway cottages. The renaming of Kingstown Street may have been based on the establishment of Kingston, Jamaica, in 1872, but it may also have an Irish basis (Kingstown being a few miles to the south of Dublin), in common with other streets in the Camden area.

At the south-eastern end of Kingstown Street, we come to **PRINCESS ROAD**, whose first houses were built in the late 1840s. The street is named after either Princess Helena or Princess Louise, daughters of Queen Victoria born in 1846 and 1848. Terraces of varying quality line the street, with shops in the centre terrace on the west side. East of Chalcot Road, **No.35** was clearly a shop, since converted to domestic use. It was a haberdasher's in 1868. The old shop window remains, with a pair of doors in the middle, giving on to a sheer drop below. A gap on the canal side of the road is filled by **Primrose Hill Primary School** of 1884, typical of the Victorian Board Schools. The school playground extends behind the southern terrace on this side of the road. At the end of Princess Road is the Engineer public house and the modern (early 1970s) development, **WATERSIDE PLACE**, narrow four-storey terraced houses, with gates on to the canal towpath, built on an old brewery site.

The plot between the canal and Princess Road was bought at the 1840 Estate sale by Calverts, the brewers who also controlled the Chalk Farm Tavern.

They must have built **The Engineer** pub, which appears on the 1849 map and still stands, with a sign showing Brunel in front of the Saltash Bridge. Though he was a famous railway engineer, Robert Stephenson as the engineer of the London and Birmingham Railway would have been more appropriate. The brewery could be approached both from the canal and via an underground passage under Gloucester Avenue to the railway sidings. In the 1890s Pickfords' stables were here. The building opposite, **No.42**, was Allsop's stables, built about 1880, and is currently occupied by various parties including the London Film Makers' Co-op and the London Musicians' Collective. The underground passage led from Pickfords under the road to Allsop's, and then under the railway lines to the goods shed and Allsop's beer store. Horses were taken through this passage, which still exists except at the western end, which has been blocked off for security reasons.

Turning left from Princess Road into Gloucester Avenue we encounter a short terrace, **Nos.67-77**, originally called Waterloo Terrace, with small shops. On the right is a three-storey house, **No.44a**, originally part of the warehouse and workshop complex at **No.44**, which made up the Postal Telegraph works in the 1860s. The complex has subsequently been used as warehouses and as Druce's Furniture Store. It is now occupied by smaller firms, including a workshop for the restoration of Islamic art.

After Edis Street on the left a terrace, **No.79** onwards, shows a change in style after three houses. From this point northwards to Fitzroy Road the houses on both sides of the road (once called Lodowick Terrace on the west and Lansdowne Terrace on the east) were designed by Joseph Gandar (p 74), who named Lodowick Terrace after the principal founder of the Muggletonians (Lodowick Muggleton). Why the terrace opposite was not called after his cousin and co-founder John Reeve remains puzzling. These terraces were built in the 1850s and 60s, the space between Lansdowne Terrace and the railway being developed for commercial use with access from Dumpton Place, as described in section 4A.

From here one can either return to Chalk Farm station via the upper end of Gloucester Avenue, or return to the old Tavern Gardens via Chalcot Road, or stroll through to Primrose Hill at the far end of Fitzroy Road.

The 'York and Albany' to Primrose Hill

(see map 1 at end of book)

THE SURVEY of this area starts at the point where Parkway (the road from the Gloucester Gate of Regent's Park to Camden Town) crosses what was the canal spur leading to Cumberland Basin and then the mainline railway bridge. On the right, on the eastern corner of Park Village East, is the façade of the York and Albany, a Regency hostelry no longer in use but cutely provided with painted 'windows' behind which silhouetted figures of the 1870s appear to drink and converse.

Across Parkway from the York and Albany is the corner of Gloucester Avenue, originally called Gloucester Road. This wayward road starts by curving round to the left, almost westwards, but then makes an abrupt right half-turn at Cecil Sharp House, leaving the roadway to continue as Regent's Park Road. Gloucester Avenue now proceeds north-westwards, following the line of the railway, to abut at length onto the northern end of Regent's Park Road, which has curved round in a huge crescent. The Avenue's peculiar path at its southern end was dictated by the development of the railway line from Chalk Farm to Euston.

The area we shall be dealing with was built up almost entirely after the 1840 sale of the Southampton estate. The first building to be erected at the southern end of **GLOUCESTER AVENUE** was a private house later bought by nuns and used as a convent, Holy Rood House. In 1908 when railway tunnelling caused extensive damage, the house had to be rebuilt and at that time a chapel in romanesque style, which can be glimpsed today from Prince Albert Road, was added at the back. In the 1970s the nuns built a smaller, more practical centre ('Centrepeace') at **No.3** and the main house became, first, the Japanese School for London and in the late 1980s Northbridge House School, which uses the chapel as its assembly hall.

At one time there were some large villas on the other side of Gloucester Avenue, beyond the junction with Oval Road. These were actually built before 1840 (but after the coming of the railway), probably by Henry Bassett, then a young and promising architect. He was born about 1803 and died young in 1846. The Bassett family were surveyors to the Southampton Estate, and Henry's father and later his brother, both named George, lived in one of these villas, appropriately called Southampton Lodge. George Bassett Jr had bought plots on both sides of the road, some 4½ acres, for nearly £1950; this was considerably more than the average price of about £300 an acre. The 1861 Census shows that George Bassett was 60 and his wife Katherine 48. Their household consisted of four daughters and a son, ranging in age from 6 to 11, with a nurse and nursemaid, cook and housemaid.

Next to the present Convent is a pair of villas, **Nos.7 and 9**. The left-hand one was rebuilt between the wars to a greater height. Then comes **No.11**, a red-brick replacement of a detached house bombed in WW II, followed by **Nos.15-31**, a neat terrace of 1848-9, boasting privet hedges to all the tiny front gardens. Antoine Claudet, well known in photographic circles of his time as a great innovator, lived in **No.21** until his death in 1867. In the 1861 Census, when he was 63, his household included his wife, mother-in-law of 93, a daughter of 30, three grandsons and three maidservants. The Claudets and Bassetts are good examples of the well-to-do, multi-offspring, mid-Victorian families in this new neighbourhood.

A pair of villas, **Nos.33 and 35**, follows. In the first, now much altered and extended, lived Joseph Guerrier, builder and developer in several streets of this area in the 1840s. The next pair, although originally numbered in with Gloucester Road, are now in Regent's Park Road, as is Cecil Sharp House on the other side, so more of them later. The old **lamp standards** in Gloucester Avenue are noteworthy; some of them have on their doors in relief the arms of St Pancras Borough, while others have the earlier Vestry seal, showing an effigy of St Pancras, the boy martyr, trampling on a Roman soldier who brandishes a sword.

We now turn right into the part of Gloucester Avenue running northwards along the line of the railway. The plots on both sides of the Avenue up to St Mark's Crescent (George Bassett's purchase, including the site of the present Cecil Sharp House) were developed by about 1851-52. All the west-side houses in this stretch have survived except one, which has been replaced by a block of modern flats, **No.41**. In **No.57** lived from 1860 onwards Thomas Jones Barker, a painter of historical and battle scenes.

On the east side were until recent times some splendid villas by Henry Bassett. In 1971 approval for their demolition was rushed through by Camden Council, in spite of protests by local residents, backed by the Victorian Society and various other people of distinction. The villas were replaced by the present Darwin Court flats. This incident had one fortunate outcome: it caused the creation of the Primrose Hill Conservation Area, which covers all of this section and parts of Section 3 as well.

It may seem odd that such grand villas were built along the railway. However, one must remember that in 1840 there were only four tracks, much farther from the houses, and the trains were rope-hauled past here for the next few years. Residents in these villas included Henry Courtney Selous, the artist, who lived in **No.28** from the 1850s to the 1880s, but died in Devon in 1890. His large painting of Queen Victoria opening the Great Exhibition in the Crystal Palace on 1 May 1851 is in the permanent collection of the Victoria and Albert Museum. Next door at **No.26** lived Frederick Courtney Selous, who was born in 1851, probably in this house. He survived the skating disaster in Regent's Park in 1867, when the ice gave way and 40 people died, and lived to acquire notoriety for his big-game hunting and political exploits in Southern Africa. He was killed there in 1917; the Selous Game Reserve in central Tanzania still commemorates his name. (Selous Street, outside our area but in Camden Town, was renamed Nelson Mandela Street in the 1970s.) Charles Dickens junior, the eldest son of the author, was living here near his mother in 1870 when his father died at Gadshill.

The next house to the north was displaced by an electrical **substation** around 1960, a fate which befell the next eight houses when the suburban railway was electrified in 1910. The earlier substation faces the end of **St MARK'S CRESCENT**, which runs on the east side of the canal, with terraces and a number of semi-detached houses of the 1840s at the south end, and of the 1850s at the north. The canal-side houses have delightful gardens down to the water, with private mooring (opposite). This street has housed many artists, notably the vorticist and cubist William Roberts, who died in 1980: he was an official War Artist in both World Wars and lived in **No.14**. More recent residents include the historian A J P Taylor, the trade union leader Clive Jenkins, and Lord St Davids, founder of the Pirate Castle (p 50).

The bridge over the canal, called **Fitzroy Bridge** (after the Fitzroy family) marked the end of the original Gloucester Road. On the far side of the bridge the road, originally continuing as Southampton Road, was started very close to the railway boundary, but the railway, newly become the London and North Western, required an extra strip of land in 1846. As this took nearly the whole of the road down to the canal, the road was re-sited in its present

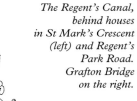

The Regent's Canal, behind houses in St Mark's Crescent (left) and Regent's Park Road. Grafton Bridge on the right.

position at the railway's expense. (For consequences at the other end of Gloucester Avenue, see p 81).

Steps beside the bridge provide access to the canal towpath, which affords an enjoyable canal-side walk westwards to Regent's Park opposite the gardens of St Mark's Crescent, or eastwards to Camden Lock (p 49). Retracing our steps a little and turning right through St Mark's Crescent, we reach Regent's Park Road again at **No.30**, in the part that was originally called Queen's Road, running east from St Mark's Square. This

developed as semi-detached villas on the south side and terraces on the north in a pleasant classical, early Victorian style, slightly spoilt by later additions. **No.15** was the home in 1897 of Sir Alexander Campbell MacKenzie, Scottish composer, who was principal of the Royal Academy of Music at the time. **No.10**, once 30 Queen's Road, was destroyed by bombing in WW II and was replaced by a small block of flats designed by Ernö Goldfinger.

The important building at the end of this road is **Cecil Sharp House**. It is built on the triangular site where Regent's Park Road and Gloucester Avenue meet, and is numbered as 2 Regent's Park Road. The site was acquired in the late 1920s by the English Folk Dance Society and their neo-Georgian building, designed by H M Fletcher, was opened in 1930. It contained Cecil Sharp's library, which he had bequeathed to the Society. Cecil James Sharp was born in London in 1859. His musical career started in Cambridge and Australia, and he was principal of the Hampstead Conservatoire of Music (in Eton Avenue) from 1896 to 1905. He became interested in traditional music and in 1902 he published *A Book of British Song* and, in 1904, *Folk Songs from Somerset*. He joined the committee of the Folk Song Society in 1904 and founded the English Folk Dance Society in 1911. The two Societies amalgamated in 1932 and became the English Folk Dance and Song Society. Cecil Sharp's search for English folk songs and dances led him as far as the Appalachian Mountains, where descendants of a group of English settlers lived, and he noted altogether some 5000 tunes and variants. He died in 1924.

The building was badly damaged by a bomb in September 1940 but, after first-aid repairs, was made usable until rebuilding was at last possible in 1949. An extra storey was added, but the most interesting feature was the replacement of the former musicians' gallery in the main hall by a vast mural painting by Ivon Hitchens nearly 70 feet long, completed in June 1954.

Turning now at Cecil Sharp House and walking back up the south (odd-numbered) side of Regent's Park Road, we encounter between **Nos. 3** and **5** the entrance to **REGAL LANE**. This started life as Queen's Mews, so called because it served Queen's Road. It runs behind the Regent's Park Road and Gloucester Avenue houses, and immediately behind the grand houses of Prince Albert Road, to the back of the school buildings where we started. Although minor, it was one of the roads which were laid down by the Southampton Estate before the 1840 sale. In 1937 the name of Queen's Mews was changed to Regal Mews and then to Regal Lane. On one side only (the other side being formed of the back walls of Prince Albert Road houses or their gardens) are some 1960s houses in a semi-rural setting.

Further west along Regent's Park Road we come to the hump in the road which marks the bridge, named **Grafton Bridge** after another Fitzroy family name, over the canal which has taken a sharp turn at Prince Albert Road and is now making for Camden Lock. It is still of the original brickwork, strengthened internally with concrete in the late 1960s (like Fitzroy Bridge more recently). The road now becomes one side of the so-called **St MARK'S SQUARE**, which has houses only on two sides. This could have been three-quarters of a square if **St Mark's Church** had not occupied the central site.

By the mid-1840s, the need for a church to serve the new building development had become apparent and a temporary church was opened in 1848 on the site of the present **36 Regent's Park Road** and **4 St Mark's Square**. This had '600 sittings' (places), of which 150 were free; those were the days when one paid a pew rent for one's place in church. The site for the new church, bought in 1840 by the Crown, was presented by its architect, Thomas Little, according to his obituary in *The Builder*, but it is perhaps more likely that he gave (or lent) the site for the temporary church, which was built on his plot. Documents in the Heal Collection at the Local Studies Library imply that he was one of several contributors to the cost of the main site. However, enough money was collected by 1851 for the foundation stone to be laid by Dr Thomas Dale, the vicar of St Pancras. The nave and aisles were finished and consecrated in 1853 by Bishop Blomfield, and his son, Sir Arthur Blomfield, an architect of some renown, completed the chancel in 1891. Booth's Survey of 1902 refers to the 'extreme High Church practices' at St Mark's. The church was badly bombed in 1940 and acquired another temporary church in 1943 - a hut in the garden. The war damage was not repaired until 1956-7 under the direction of Sir Ninian Comper, who at age 93 was present at the re-consecration. His new reredos replaced the original, which he had installed in 1938.

The houses on the west side of St Mark's Square are semi-detached villas of asymmetrical design, completed by 1849. The north side is a more conventional terrace of about 1860, now a **nurses' home**, with columniated porticoes in which most of the old front doors have become windows.

On the north side of Regent's Park Road, the plots between Princess Road and Fitzroy Road were bought at the 1840 sale by Thomas Little, the architect of St Mark's Church, so it is possible that he was the designer of some, if not all, of the houses in this stretch. They include the homes of some well-known former residents. **No.48** was the home of the

novelist Nigel Balchin, who lived here from 1960 until his death in 1970. On the other side of the road, Dr Ludwig Friedburger lived in **No.41**, where Friedrich Engels died in 1895 (p 77). The even numbers, **Nos.36-64**, continue westwards mostly as linked semi-detached houses, first occupied by comfortably-off professional or retired people, and include two nice detached (or nearly detached) villas, **Nos. 58** and **60**. The three closest to Fitzroy Road were first occupied in 1849, and all were finished down to St Mark's Square by 1850-60.

No.62, one of a pair rather larger than the rest, was occupied by Mary Angela Dickens in the 1890s. She was the daughter of the author's eldest son, Charles, who had lived in Gloucester Avenue, and was herself a novelist; but who knows *A Mere Cypher* and her other works now? The actor Henry Ainley had the house from 1915 to 1921. **No.68** had a fictional existence in a novel called *The Hiding Place*, by the actor Robert Shaw: it is not quite the same house, but he admitted he made it up because he once lived in **No.66**. A real dweller in No.68 was Dr Jonathan Miller, now well known as a stage director, who started his married life here in 1956. **No.70** at one time had the name Sandhurst Lodge on the gate posts. It was first occupied by Captain Thomas Malkin, who had previously lived in No.1, Regent's Park Road, also called Sandhurst

Lodge. He was an army crammer, so took the name of this house with him when he moved. In 1851 he had six young gentlemen 'studying the military profession' staying with him.

On the odd-numbered side of the road we encounter the two-ended **ALBERT TERRACE MEWS**, now mostly lined with smart little houses, which originally served the block between St Mark's Square and Albert Terrace. The houses on the far (west) side of the mews and in the south-west corner are original service cottages, somewhat altered; the rest is modern work, built in the old back gardens.

Round the corner and with a handsome view of Primrose Hill, **ALBERT TERRACE** was developed as three pairs of grand semi-detached villas (p 86), once with an attractive large house called Mymm's Villa on the corner with Prince Albert Road. This was replaced in the 1960s by a block of flats, not too overpowering for the site but faced with aggressive red bricks alien to this stucco and stock brick area. Prince Albert of Saxe-Coburg-Gotha married Queen Victoria in February 1840, 6 months before the Southampton sale, so it is not surprising to find his name given to various streets and roads in the neighbourhood.

In **No.2 Albert Terrace** Roger Fenton, famous photographer of the Crimean War, was living in 1851 with his wife and two small daughters. He was a versatile person variously described as barrister, painter, landscape and portrait photographer.

We know from records of the committee organising the building of St Mark's temporary church that **No.4** of the terrace was not quite finished in 1848.

PRINCE ALBERT ROAD was called Primrose Hill Road when Regent's Park was completed, but acquired the name Albert Road soon after Queen Victoria's marriage; it was so called in Wells' *The War of the Worlds*. The 'Prince' was not added until 1937, when the LCC tried to reduce the number of Albert Streets and Roads which then abounded. In a temporary wooden shed at the foot of the Hill along this road was carved the monument to Queen Victoria which stands in front of Buckingham Palace. An area of about one-fifth of an acre was railed off in the early 1900s to form a studio for the sculptor, Thomas Brock, then living in Osnaburgh Street. It took him 9 years, and he was knighted by King George V at the unveiling of the memorial on 16 May 1911.

The north part of the Zoo is on the other side of the road, but as the Zoo is unable to man the convenient north gates opposite the end of Albert Terrace, these are permanently closed. The boundary between St Pancras and St Marylebone parishes used to cut half-way down Primrose Hill and through the middle of the Zoo, but has been adjusted to bring all of Primrose Hill into Camden and all of the Zoo into Westminster.

After the red brick flats, **No.23**, there are three pairs of symmetrical villas at **Nos.22-17**, still largely unspoilt and showing some interesting detail, including central medallions between pairs of houses, although of course they have different owners. Then comes **No.16** on the corner of St Mark's Square: this in the 1930s was the home of the Waters family, of stage and radio fame. Elsie and Doris were perhaps better known as Gert and Daisy and their brother, Jack Warner, changed

Late 1840s houses in Albert Terrace (No. 2 on left)

his surname for professional purposes. He was married from this house in St Mark's Church.

Water Meeting Bridge over the canal comes after the church and is so called because here was the junction of the main canal and the branch down to Cumberland Market. (In "Some Recollections of Mortality", a chapter of *The Uncommercial Traveller,* Charles Dickens muses over an incident, which he obviously witnessed precisely at this spot, of the callousness of local bystanders towards the body of a woman who had drowned in the canal nearby.) The traffic on this stretch of road was too much for the original brick bridge and it was completely rebuilt and widened in 1961.

Beyond the bridge comes a row of elegant stuccoed villas painted the uniform cream which indicates Crown Estate. The early history of these, **Nos.1-15 PRINCE ALBERT ROAD**, is bound up with that of Regent's Park Road and Joseph Guerrier in particular. A slight bulge in the boundary of Marylebone Park left a small strip of Crown land to the north of the smooth curve of Nash's road; this strip tapered from about 50 feet wide at the Parkway end to almost nothing at Water Meeting Bridge. There was just enough room to build a few houses tight up to the north boundary at the eastern end and **Nos.1-5** were built like this. Then it would appear that the Crown did a deal with

Peter Pearse and Joseph Guerrier, who had bought the plots north of the boundary. Regal Lane, then Queen's Mews, was partly realigned, and the southern half of the long plots on which the present Nos.5-33 Regent's Park Road stand were conveyed to the Crown, thus providing enough depth for more houses to be built. **Nos.6-15** Prince Albert Road are on these sites; No.9 was rebuilt in the 1980s after lying in bomb ruins since WW II. Leases of up to 99 years on the Crown sites, including those at the eastern end, were granted to Guerrier and Pearse, presumably as part of the agreement, so it is likely that they built the houses concerned. Apart from **Nos.3-4**, the home of the Nuffield Provincial Hospitals Trust, most of the house leases are again in private hands, as they were originally.

In 1912 there was a complaint from the occupants of **No.3** that the General Omnibus Company's vehicles shook the house – so could they not be diverted to join the others which ran down Regent's Park Road? **No.2** housed the Ranee of Sarawak in 1930 and the actress Tallulah Bankhead lived in **No.10** for about a year in the 1930s. **No.4** has an extension on the east side, consisting of a studio with two small bedrooms over it, designed by E (later Sir Edward) Brantwood Maufe in 1913 for the then lessee, A E Maude, the artist. During the tenancy of Mr Henry Bruce in the late 1920s, the studio seems

to have been used for practice by his wife, the world-famous ballerina, Tamara Karsavina. The house was run as a wartime day nursery by the St Pancras Borough Council in 1943 and was then taken over by the LCC. The Crown recovered vacant possession in 1969.

At the corner of Prince Albert Road with Parkway we have come full circle, more or less at the centre of the area surveyed, and within sight of the nearest Nash terrace in Regent's Park, beyond the entrance at Gloucester Gate. From here one is within a few yards of almost any of the sections described and could strike east to gaze again upon the Nash terraces or penetrate the area that used to serve them; south into Delancey Street and hence Mornington Terrace to the old Carreras factory and beyond, to the ultra-modern Euston Centre; west down to one of the most historic sites, Old Mother Red Cap in Camden High Street, hard by a far newer development, Camden Lock with its Interchange Building; or north to another of the oldest sites, the Chalk Farm Tavern.

Truly, this must be one of the most interesting, and varied, parts of London, with its rich mix of elegant residential, commercial and industrial buildings, served by restaurants, pubs, cinemas and theatres, and lived in and loved by a multitude of artists and musicians, writers and philosophers.

Sources

Abercrombie, Patrick & Foreshaw, J H. *County of London plan* (Macmillan, 1943)

Baron, Wendy. *The Camden Town Group* (Scolar Press, 1979)

Bebbington, Gillian. *London street names* (Batsford, 1972)

Booth, Charles. *Life & labour of the people in London* (Macmillan, 1892-7)

Clarke, Basil. *Parish churches of London* (Batsford, 1966)

Department of the Environment. *List of buildings of special architectural or historic interest as at 14 May 1974, London Borough of Camden* (DOE, 1974)

Dickens, Charles. *Dickens' dictionary of London...*(Charles Dickens, 18??)

Elmes, James & Shepherd, Thomas H. *Metropolitan improvements...*(Jones, 1827)

Gernsheim H, & Gernsheim A. *L J M Daguerre: the history of the diorama and daguerrotype.* 2nd ed (NewYork: Dover, 1968)

Graves, Algernon. *The Royal Academy of Arts: a complete dictionary...1769 to 1904* (H Graves; George Bell, 1905-6)

Horne, M A C. *The Northern Line: a short history* (Rose, 1987)

Howard, Diana. *London theatres and music halls 1850-1950* (Library Assoc, 1970)

Kinross, F. *Breaking the ice: frozen deliveries.* In *Country Life*, 18.10.1990

Mansbridge, Michael. *John Nash: a complete catalogue* (Phaidon, 1991)

Miller, Frederick. *St Pancras past and present* (Abel Heywood, 1874)

Nelson, Sarah. *The history of Camden Goods Yard* (Unpublished typescript, 1986?)

New, Michael. *The Regent's Canal: a study of development, Hampstead Road Bridge to Water Meeting Junction* (Unpublished thesis, 1992)

Norris, Gerald. *A musical gazetteer of Great Britain & Ireland* (David & Charles, 1981)

Palmer, Samuel. *St Pancras...* (Samuel Palmer, 1870)

Pevsner, Nikolaus. *London, except the cities of London and Westminster* (Penguin, 1952). *(The buildings of England)*

Richardson, John. *Camden Town and Primrose Hill past* (Historical Pubns, 1991)

Richardson, John. *A Camden Town walk* (Camden History Society, 1978)

Rottmann, Alexander. *London Catholic churches* (Sands, 1926)

Royal Commission on London Squares. *Report* (HMSO, 1928). Cmd 3196

St Pancras (Metropolitan Borough). *Official handbook* (Pyramid Press, 1957)

Saunders, Ann. *Regent's Park* (David & Charles, 1969)

Sickert, Walter. *A free house! or, The artist as craftsman* (Macmillan, 1947)

Survey of London, Vols. XIX and XXI (London County Council, 1938 & 1949)

Wainwright, David. *The piano-makers* (Hutchinson, 1975)

Walford, Edward. *Old and new London.* Vol.5 (Cassell, c1880)

Webster, A D. *Regent's Park & Primrose Hill* (Greening, 1911)

Wheatley, Henry Benjamin. *London past and present* (John Murray, 1891)

Williams, George G. *Guide to literary London* (Batsford, 1973)

Williams, Thomas J. & Campbell, A W. *The Park Village sisterhood* (SPCK, 1965)

Biographical

Ackroyd, Peter. *Dickens* (Sinclair-Stevenson, 1990)
Noakes, Vivien, *Edward Lear: the life of a wanderer* (BBC, 1985)
Holroyd, Michael. *Bernard Shaw, Vol. 1* (Chatto, 1988)
Weintraub, Stanley. *Four Rossettis: a Victorian biography* (W H Allen. 1978)
The dictionary of national biography
Who was who

Maps

London & Environs

1746	Rocque
1792-99	Horwood
1828	Greenwood
1840	Ruff
1862	Stanford
1862	Waller
1866-71	Ordnance Survey (and later)
1889-98	Booth's Poverty Maps

St Pancras

1804	Thompson
1839	Davies, B R
1849	Daw (and later to 1880)

Goad's Insurance Maps

Other Sources

Camden History Review,
  Nos 2, 3, 6, 7, 8, 9, 18

The Hampstead & Highgate Express;
Camden Journal; St Pancras Journal

Camden Local Studies Library,
  including the Heal Collection

The Guildhall Library
Westminster City Libraries
RIBA Library

LCC Street Lists
  and GLC Street Naming Section
Post Office and street directories
Rate books

Census returns
Planning applications
Southampton Papers
  (Greater London Records Office)
The Drinking Fountain Association

Diorama Arts
Father Markey (St Mary Magdalene)
Elain Harwood (English Heritage)

Index

Streets included
in the survey
are indicated in
boldface, as is the
main entry for each.
Asterisks denote
illustrations.